FLAVORS of IRELAND

Celebrating Grand Places and Glorious Food

FLAVORS  of IRELAND

Celebrating Grand Places and Glorious Food

Margaret M. Johnson

FOREWORD BY
NOEL MCMEEL

Best Chef, Ulster, 2011

Ambassador International
GREENVILLE, SOUTH CAROLINA & BELFAST, NORTHERN IRELAND

www.ambassador-international.com

Flavors of Ireland

Celebrating Grand Places and Glorious Food

ISBN: 978-1-935507-79-6

Printed in China

Cover Design & Page Layout by David Siglin

Ambassador International
Emerald House
427 Wade Hampton Blvd.
Greenville, SC 29609, USA
www.ambassador-international.com

Ambassador Books
The Mount
2 Woodstock Link
Belfast, BT6 8DD, Northern Ireland, UK
www.ambassador-international.com

The colophon is a trademark of Ambassador

Cover Photos:
Top photo courtesy of Solis Lough Eske Castle
Bottom photo courtesy of Kerryogld

DEDICATION

To my husband, Carl,
for his continued indulgence
in all things Irish.

MARGARET Johnson has done a tremendous job of bringing both traditional and new Irish cuisine to the palettes of food lovers everywhere. Her cookbook captures the essence of Irish cuisine while also revealing a genuine enthusiasm for the culture and heritage of Ireland itself.

—MICHAEL P. QUINLIN
President, Boston Irish Tourism Association

YOU'LL find plenty of golden oldies in Margaret M. Johnson's beautifully illustrated book of Irish recipes, but it's the reflection of Ireland's vibrant, contemporary food culture that really shines. Like a foodie magpie, she's picked precious jewels of culinary modernity from across this fertile island and framed them in a book of real style.

—ROSS GOLDEN-BANNON
Editor, FOOD & WINE Magazine; Restaurant Critic, The Sunday Business Post

MARGARET M. Johnson is a master storyteller and delights in all things Irish. She has brought together many of Ireland's top chefs (and their fabulous cuisine) with historical and delicious Irish favorites from her vast research. You will be transported direct to Ireland and will be cooking from Irish kitchens by the time you finish reading this wonderful book.

—ROSEANN TULLY
CEO & Founder, Intermezzo Magazine

MARGARET Johnson's *Flavors of Ireland* will take you on a mouth-watering culinary tour of Ireland, as the Irish know it. The author has a deep acquaintance with Ireland and is entirely on the mark in her analysis: 'No matter how much you've heard about Ireland, no matter how great your expectations, the Ireland you experience will far surpass the Ireland you imagine'. The book takes readers on a delectable journey around the best tables in Ireland today. The recipes, whether homely and traditional Irish, or 'new' Irish fine dining, are presented elegantly and simply, so all can recreate the flavors of Ireland at their own tables. The photography, of both the food and the landscape, is simply stunning.

—EMMA COWAN
Publisher, Flavour Magazine

THIS is a heartfelt book which not only makes you fall in love with Ireland but also captures the true essence of modern Irish cuisine.

—MARGARET JEFFARES
Founder and Managing Director, Good Food Ireland

WESTERN IRELAND

SOUTHERN IRELAND

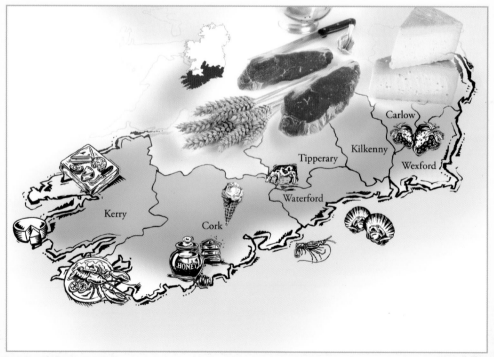

Northern Ireland

Eastern Ireland

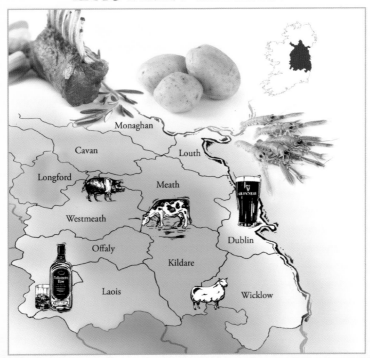

Map courtesy of Tourism Ireland

TABLE OF CONTENTS

FOREWORD

IT is a great pleasure for me to introduce this book by my friend Margaret Johnson. Since we first met in 1998 at the James Beard Foundation in New York—I was cooking, she was reporting—Margaret has continually been in the pursuit of showcasing modern Irish food on a world stage.

A lot has changed from the great famine of the 1850s. For decades, most Irish cooking has been thought of as a "one-pot wonder," with Irish Stew being one of the best examples. Not that there's anything wrong with a good Irish Stew, but times have changed in Ireland, and Margaret has always been a champion of that change. When you take a tour of this book, you'll know what I mean!

Happiness is meant to be shared and, thankfully, many classically trained chefs from around the world are working in Ireland with great technique, great passion, and a great willingness to share good recipes. Thankfully too, Margaret has compiled some of the best in this book.

Good food depends entirely on good ingredients, and as a chef myself, I try to source the best ones and put them in the right recipe. If you like to cook, you're halfway there. This book of recipes reflects an Irish culture that has changed tremendously over the years, but the one thing that has not changed is the absolute obsession for and love of preparation of great local food. Like most chefs here, we not only take an interest in our work, we are proud of what we do and what we have to work with in Ireland.

Recipes tell you about a people—how they live, how they eat, and what foods are special to them. *Flavors of Ireland* offers you an opportunity to come to the table and enjoy these qualities with them.

Noel McMeel, Executive Chef
Lough Erne Resort
Enniskillen, Co. Fermanagh

SLIABH LUACHRA DRIVE

AODHGHAN O RATHAILLE-
A AIT BREITHE
(BIRTHPLACE)

SLIABH LUACHRA DRIVE

EOGHAN RUA O SUILLEABHAIN-
A BHAILE
(HOME)

ACKNOWLEDGMENTS

I'D like to express thanks to my friend, Noel McMeel, and to the countless chefs, hotels, restaurants, and food producers who contributed recipes and photographs to this book. I would also like to acknowledge the support of Tourism Ireland (Irish Tourist Board), Bord Bia (Irish Food Board), Good Food Ireland, and these sponsors:

BEWLEY IRISH IMPORTS
Importer of Irish Giftware and Food
Lakeshore Mustard, Mileeven Honey,
Bewleys Coffee and Tea, and Crossogue Preserves
and Curds

CASTLE BRANDS INC.
Importer of Knappogue Castle 12 Year Old Irish Whiskey,
Clontarf 1014 Irish Whiskey,
Boru Vodka, Celtic Honey, and Brady's Irish Cream

CELTIC GOLF & QUINLAN TOURS
Distinctive Travel Experiences in
Ireland, England, Scotland, and Wales

KERRYGOLD/IRISH DAIRY BOARD
Importer of Irish Butter and Cheese
Dubliner, Blarney Castle, Cheddar, Swiss, Red Leicester,
Ivernia, Duhallow, Dubliner with Stout, and
Cheddar with Whiskey

LILY O'BRIEN'S CHOCOLATE CAFE
Original Irish Chocolate Café
in the Heart of Midtown Manhattan

LOUGH ERNE RESORT
Enniskillen, Co. Fermanagh
The Ultimate Expression in Old World Heritage
and New World Luxury

MAGNERS IRISH CIDER
Producer of Irish Cider
Original Apple and Pear

SOLIS LOUGH ESKE CASTLE
Donegal Town
Luxury Country Hotel and Spa Steeped in History

STURM FOODS
Importer of McCann's Irish Oatmeal

TOMMY MOLONEY'S IRISH MEATS
Producer of Traditional Irish Meats,
Bacon and Pork Products, and Corned Beef

INTRODUCTION

The great masterpieces of Irish food arrive at the table as a blessing
of the Irish climate, the Irish countryside, and the Irish people.
Travel the country eating the local specialties, and you can discover,
through these transfixing tastes, a true sense of the place where you are.

JOHN AND SALLY MCKENNA
"The Irish Table," *Bon Appetit*, May 1996

No matter how much you've heard about Ireland, no matter how great your expectations, the Ireland you experience will far surpass the Ireland you imagine.

You expect grand sights like the drama of the Dingle Peninsula and the wildness of Connemara. The mysteries of Celtic history beckon to be explored in places like Newgrange in Meath's Boyne Valley, at Glendalough in the heart of Wicklow, and on the Giant's Causeway along the Antrim coast. The dolmen-dotted Midlands, the hairpin turns of Kerry's Ring, and the elegant squares of Georgian Dublin are all part of the expected pleasures of an Irish holiday.

Alongside Ireland's scenic splendor, in fact even beyond its stunning landscape, are the special pleasures of Irish food. In a country not always known for its culinary greatness yet long praised for its hospitality and tradition of sharing food with family, friends, and strangers, Ireland has developed into a land where the culinary arts are being recognized among the best in Europe.

When I first visited Ireland more than twenty-five years ago, I embraced both its grand places and its glorious food. I fell in love with the place where my grandparents and great-grandparents were born. I loved the people, the pubs, the landscape, the history, the folklore, and the music.

I loved the wooly, black-faced sheep, the languid cows, the peat-filled bogs, and the thatch-covered cottages.

I loved Ireland's traditional foods—big, meaty breakfasts, bowls of soup and stew, and sandwiches made with thick slabs of ham and slices of cheddar cheese. Over the years, I've enjoyed a tipple or two of Ireland's legendary drinks as well—creamy pints of Guinness, glasses of golden whiskey, and silky cream liqueurs. In truth, there wasn't much I didn't love about Ireland—then and now—and fifty visits later, the love affair continues.

I like to think I grew with Ireland's food "revolution"—the period from the early 1980s when Irish cooks came to realize that they had some of the best natural ingredients, literally, at their doorsteps: luscious beef, lamb, pork, poultry, fresh fish, incomparable dairy products, wild fruits and berries, and vegetables, especially the beloved potato, the country's great staple. After exploring Irish cookery in five previous cookbooks, I can honestly say Irish food grows more fascinating with every bite.

Flavors of Ireland will show you how its food, often used in Irish literature to provide focus, punctuation, rhythm, and, in some instances, entire plots, has moved boldly into the twenty-first century—no longer, as James Joyce once wrote, "an outcast from life's feast."

With more than seventy inspired recipes in five chapters—wonderful breads and scones for breakfast and tea; appetizing starters like smoked cheese soup and mussels steamed in Guinness; classic stews and fashionable tarts; hearty main courses of local lamb, pork, beef, and seafood; and decadent desserts ranging from steamed puddings and fruity crumbles to creamy cheesecakes and elegant tarts—*Flavors of Ireland* offers exciting dishes from traditional and trendy Ireland and deliciously defines Irish cooking today. *Bain taitneamh as do bhéile! Bon appétit!*

A Note on the Recipes

For all the recipes, quantities are expressed in standard cups and spoons as well as in metric measurements. Cooks should follow one set, not a mixture of both.

When a recipe calls for bacon, either conventional American bacon or Irish-style bacon (also called "rashers," "back bacon," and "Irish breakfast bacon") is noted. When cooked, Irish bacon will not be crisp like American bacon because it contains 65% less fat. For American readers, Tommy Moloney's brand of Irish bacon is suggested.

When a recipe calls for butter, salted or unsalted Kerrygold Irish butter is recommended. Because it's sold in 8 oz./225 g packages, quantities are expressed in tablespoons (16 tbsp. per package). When a recipe calls for oatmeal, McCann's Irish Oatmeal is recommended. When a recipe calls for whiskey, Knappogue Castle Single Malt is recommended.

Vegetables and fruits are standard size and are washed and peeled before using unless otherwise noted. Apples and pears are generally peeled, cored, and sliced. When a recipe calls for "baking apples" for pies, tarts, and cakes, a mixture of Granny Smith, Rome Beauty, and Newton Pippin provides exceptional flavor. When a recipe calls for "eating apples" for sauces and compotes, try Braeburn, Cortland, Jonagold, McIntosh, or Winesap. Two Irish varieties are also highly recommended for cooking: Bramley, an heirloom variety prized for its balance of sugar and acid, and Cox's Orange Pippin, considered the benchmark for flavor in apples. Two large apples are equivalent to about 1 pound. Anjou, Bartlett, and Bosc pears are preferred for baking since they're juicy and hold their shape. Red Bartlett and Red Anjou are similar in flavor and texture but are more colorful and a bit more expensive. Three pears are equivalent to about 1 pound.

Photo courtesy of Bord Bia

BREAKFAST, BRUNCH, BREADS

Breakfast was over in the boarding house and the table of the breakfast-room was covered with plates on which lay yellow streaks of eggs with morsels of bacon fat and bacon rind. Mrs. Mooney sat in the straw arm-chair and watched the servant Mary remove the breakfast things. She made Mary collect the crusts and pieces of broken bread to help to make Tuesday's bread-pudding.

JAMES JOYCE
Dubliners

FULL IRISH

IF there's one meal that sets Ireland apart from all other places, it's a Full Irish: a super-hearty bacon and eggs dish that was once known as a "farmhouse breakfast." Certainly hearty enough to keep an Irish farmer well nourished through a morning's work, this dish's term is no longer completely accurate since folks in every kitchen in Ireland—from castles in Clare to hotels in Dublin—pride themselves on serving (and eating) what has become the benchmark of Irish hospitality. The traditional Irish breakfast, also called a "fry," includes eggs, bacon (rashers), sausages (bangers), black and white puddings, potatoes, grilled mushrooms and tomatoes, sometimes beans, sometimes lamb's kidneys, and any number of homemade breads and muffins. Health-conscious natives might save this indulgence for a weekend brunch or holiday, but it's safe to say visitors almost never say "no thanks" to an Irish breakfast. For an "Ulster Fry," serve this with Fadge (see Variation).

- 8 slices Irish breakfast bacon
- 2 tbsp. salted Irish butter
- 4 Irish sausages
- 4 slices black breakfast pudding
- 4 slices white breakfast pudding
- 2 medium tomatoes, halved
- 8 medium white mushrooms
- 4 to 8 large eggs

1. In a large skillet over medium heat, cook the rashers, turning frequently, for 7–9 minutes or until lightly browned. Transfer to a large platter and keep warm.
2. Melt 1 tbsp. of the butter in the same skillet. Cook the sausages and pudding slices, turning frequently, for 5–7 minutes or until browned on all sides. Transfer to platter with bacon.
3. Add the tomatoes, cut-side down, and cook for 3–4 minutes or until warm. Transfer to platter with bacon and sausages. Add the mushrooms to the skillet and cook for 4–5 minutes or until tender. Transfer to platter with bacon, sausages, and tomatoes.
4. Add the remaining tbsp. of butter to skillet. Fry eggs (1 or 2 per person) for 4–6 minutes (or to preference).
5. To serve, arrange eggs on 4 plates and surround with meats, tomatoes, and mushrooms.

VARIATION: ULSTER FRY WITH FADGE

COOK the bacon, eggs, sausage, puddings, tomatoes, and mushrooms as in a Full Irish and add this potato bread from Robert Ditty's bakery in Castledawson, Co. Londonderry, for a Northern Irish breakfast plate.

1. In a medium bowl, combine 1 cup/225 g mashed potatoes, 1/4 cup/60 g all-purpose flour, 1 tbsp. melted Irish butter, and pinch of salt. Knead into a dough (add additional flour to make a pliable dough).
2. Turn out onto a lightly floured surface and either pat or roll the mixture to a 1/2-inch/1 cm-thick round. With a 3 inch/7.5 cm biscuit cutter, cut into about 4 potato cakes.
3. In a large skillet over medium-high heat, heat 1 tbsp. canola oil.
4. Add potato cakes and cook on each side for 3–5 minutes or until browned.
5. Serve immediately or make ahead and transfer to a baking sheet and keep warm in a 250°F/130°C oven.

Makes 4 potato cakes

SCRAMBLED EGGS WITH SMOKED SALMON AND BOXTY

This special occasion breakfast or brunch dish is often served with champagne, Buck's Fizz (half champagne/half orange juice), or Black Velvet (half champagne/half Guinness), but a cup of coffee or tea works equally well. The word boxty is derived from the Irish bac-staí, referring to the traditional cooking of potatoes on the hob (bac) over an open fire (staí). The most popular recipe uses a combination of grated raw and cooked mashed potatoes that are patted together as small cakes and then fried. Variations, however, are numerous, and the little cakes can be served for breakfast or as a side dish for lunch or dinner.

- 2 large baking potatoes, peeled
- 2 large eggs, beaten
- 1/2 tsp. salt
- 1/2 tsp. freshly ground pepper
- pinch of ground nutmeg
- 3 tbsp. all-purpose flour
- 2–4 tbsp. salted Irish butter for frying
- scrambled eggs for serving
- 12 slices smoked salmon for topping
- crème fraîche for serving
- lemon wedges for serving
- chopped fresh chives for garnish

1. Cut 1 potato into 1 1/2 inch/3.5 cm pieces and cook in boiling salted water for 12–15 minutes or until tender. Drain and mash.
2. Line a large bowl with a piece of muslin, cheesecloth, or a clean linen towel. Using the large holes of a box grater, grate the other potato into a bowl. Squeeze the cloth to extract as much of the starchy liquid as possible and then discard the liquid.
3. Combine the mashed potatoes and grated potatoes and stir in the eggs, salt, pepper, and nutmeg. Add the flour, mix well, and pat into small cakes.
4. In a large skillet over medium heat, melt 2 tbsp. of the butter. Working in batches, cook the potato cakes for 3–4 minutes on each side or until lightly browned and crisp. Transfer the cakes to a baking sheet and keep warm in a 250°F/130°C oven.
5. To serve, divide the scrambled eggs onto plates. Put 2 potato cakes on each and top with a slice of smoked salmon and a spoonful of crème fraîche. Garnish with lemon and sprinkle with chives.

NEVEN MAGUIRE'S BACON-ONION-CHEESE FRITTATA

CHEF Neven Maguire, who turned his family's rural restaurant into a national phenomenon, adds both thyme and sage to this simple bacon, eggs, and cheese breakfast dish. He counts it as one of the most popular dishes served at his MacNean House Restaurant, Blacklion, Co. Cavan, where he proudly uses only the finest local ingredients. Chef Maguire and MacNean House are perennial award-winners on the Irish and international culinary scene.

- 2 tbsp. olive oil
- 2 tbsp. unsalted Irish butter
- 3 medium onions, thinly sliced
- 6 slices Irish breakfast bacon, chopped
- 1 tsp. fresh thyme leaves
- 3 garlic cloves, crushed
- salt and freshly ground pepper to taste
- 8 large eggs, beaten
- 1/2 cup/60 g grated Kerrygold Dubliner cheese
- 1 tsp. chopped fresh sage

1. In a large skillet over medium heat, heat 1 tbsp. of the oil and the butter. Add the onions and cook, stirring constantly, for 1–2 minutes or until soft but not browned. Reduce the heat to medium-low and continue to cook, stirring frequently, for 20–25 minutes or until the onions caramelize.
2. Stir the bacon, thyme, and garlic into the onions and cook for 5–8 minutes or until the bacon is lightly browned. Transfer the onion mixture to a large bowl, stir in the bacon, and season with salt and pepper.
3. Preheat the oven to 350°F/180°C. Add the eggs, cheese, and sage to the onion mixture.
4. In a deep 9-inch/23-cm ovenproof skillet, heat the remaining oil over medium-low heat. Swirl to coat the sides of the pan. Pour in the egg mixture and cook for 6–8 minutes or until the bottom is set. Transfer the pan to the oven and cook, uncovered, for about 20 minutes or until the frittata is puffed up and golden.
5. Remove the pan from the oven, loosen the sides with a spatula, and cut into wedges. Serve warm or at room temperature.

PETER FOYNES'S
POTATO-APPLE-BUTTER BAKE

PETER Foynes is mad about Irish butter! He savors its historical contributions to the cuisine and culture of Ireland and heralds it as the signature food item of the nation. Foynes is director of the Cork Butter Museum in Cork City, probably the only museum of its kind in the world dedicated to this singular product. The museum traces the history of Irish butter through remarkable artifacts, from the 56-pound keg of 1,000-year-old butter, to ancient and modern butter-making tools. The secret to this delicious potato and apple casserole is to toss them with butter just before baking.

- 4 large baking potatoes, peeled and cut into 1 1/2 inch/3.5 cm pieces
- 4 large cooking apples, peeled, cored, and cut into 1 1/2 inch/3.5 cm pieces
- 6 slices Irish breakfast bacon, chopped
- 6 tbsp. salted Irish butter
- chopped fresh chives for garnish

1. Preheat the oven to 400°F/200°C. Lightly butter an 11x7 inch/28x18 cm ovenproof baking dish.
2. In a large pot of boiling salted water, cook the potatoes for about 8 minutes or until slightly tender. Add the apples and cook for 5 minutes longer or until the potatoes and apples are tender. Remove from the heat and drain.
3. In a large skillet over medium heat, cook the bacon for 7–9 minutes or until lightly browned. Remove and set aside.
4. Melt the butter in the same skillet, add the potatoes and apples, and toss well to coat. Cook, stirring frequently, for about 5 minutes or until lightly browned. Transfer to the prepared dish and top with the bacon. Bake for about 15 minutes or until the top is browned.
5. To serve, divide the mixture onto plates and sprinkle with chives.

GRANOLA

ROLLED oats are also a key ingredient in granola, a crunchy breakfast food baked with dried fruits and nuts. It's also delicious sprinkled over fresh fruit and topped with natural yogurt.

- 2 cups/225 g McCann's Irish oatmeal
- 1 1/4 cups/115 g shredded sweetened coconut
- 4 tbsp. pine nuts
- 4 tbsp. sliced almonds
- 4 tbsp. sunflower seeds
- 4 tbsp. sesame seeds
- 4 tbsp. flax seeds
- 5 tbsp. light brown sugar
- 5 tbsp. apple or pear nectar
- 5 tbsp. Mileeven Irish Honey or similar brand
- 4 tbsp. raisins

1. Preheat the oven to 300°F/150°C. Place the oats on a large rimmed baking sheet and bake, stirring once or twice, for 20–25 minutes or until oats are lightly toasted.
2. In a large bowl, combine the coconut, pine nuts, almonds, sunflower seeds, flax seeds, and sesame seeds.
3. In a small bowl, whisk together the brown sugar, apple or pear nectar, and honey. Stir the toasted oats into the nuts mixture. Stir the liquid mixture into the dry mixture and toss to coat evenly.
4. Spray the same cookie sheet with nonstick cooking spray. Spread the granola mixture out on the pan and bake, stirring once or twice, for 15–20 minutes or until lightly browned. (Alternately, turn off the oven and leave the mixture in the oven for up to 2 hours).
5. Remove from the oven and let cool completely. Stir in the raisins and store in an airtight container for up to 1 month.

CLANDEBOYE YOGURT WITH APPLE COMPOTE

Yogurt from Clandeboye Estate, Bangor, Co. Down, is made using milk only from a herd of pampered Holstein and Jersey cows with names like Willow, Cecilia, and Mabel. The yogurt is Northern Ireland's only locally made cows' milk yogurt and is blended by hand using traditional techniques that guarantee a rich creamy texture without high fat content. The milk is prepared and cultured very gently over 24 hours in small batches, a process that helps create an exceptional flavor and texture. Chef Liz Moore of Belle Isle Cookery School, Lisbellaw, Co. Fermanagh, uses it for this lovely breakfast dish that she serves with a sweet-tart apple compote. Prepare the yogurt and compote the day before serving; also try it with a spiced version (see Variation). Belle Isle Cookery School is a member of Good Food Ireland.

- 1 (8 oz./250 ml) carton Clandeboye Natural Yogurt or similar brand
- 1–2 tbsp. Mileeven Irish Honey or similar brand
- pinch of cinnamon
- buttered toast for serving

1. The night before serving, place clean, damp cheesecloth in a sieve over a bowl. Pour the yogurt into the sieve and let it drain in the refrigerator.
2. The next morning, pick up the sides of the cloth and shape the yogurt into a ball.
3. Carefully unwrap and place it on a serving plate. Drizzle with honey and sprinkle with cinnamon. Serve it with the compote and hot buttered toast.

APPLE COMPOTE

- 3 large cooking apples, peeled, cored, and chopped
- 1 cup/250 ml water or apple juice
- 1 tbsp. fresh lemon juice
- 3 tbsp. superfine sugar
- 1 tsp. vanilla extract

1. In a medium saucepan over medium heat, bring the apples, water or juice, lemon juice, sugar, and vanilla to a boil. Cook for 2 minutes and then reduce heat and simmer for 5–6 minutes more or until the apples are nearly tender.
2. Remove from the heat and let cool completely in the pan. (Compote will keep refrigerated for up to 3 days.)

Makes about 2 cups

VARIATION: SPICED APPLE COMPOTE

For a flavorful addition to this compote, prepare as above and add 1/4 tsp. each ground cinnamon, ground cloves, and Mixed Spice (see Note) or pumpkin pie spice.

1. To make Mixed Spice, put 1 tbsp. coriander seeds, 1 crushed cinnamon stick, 1 tsp. whole cloves, and 1 tsp. allspice berries in a spice or coffee grinder. Process until finely ground.
2. Add 1 tbsp nutmeg and 2 tsp. ginger. Mix thoroughly by hand.
3. Store in an airtight container.

COMPSEY CREAMERY MASCARPONE-STUFFED FRENCH TOAST

THE Ritz-Carlton, Powerscourt, Enniskerry, Co. Wicklow, is set amidst one of the most scenic and historic estates in Ireland. The resort showcases Palladian-style architecture and features some of the most elegant dining in the area (celebrity chef Gordon Ramsay lends his name to the resort's fine dining restaurant). For a decadent start to the day—you can skip the eggs and porridge for this—the chef spreads slices of rich brioche with mascarpone cheese made at Compsey Creamery, Mullinahone, Co. Tipperary, for a delicious Irish-style French toast. He serves it with mixed berries and a sprinkling of confectioners' sugar.

- 1 large egg
- 1 cup/250 ml milk
- 1/2 tsp. ground cinnamon
- 1/2 tsp. vanilla
- 1 tsp. granulated sugar
- 4 tbsp. Compsey Creamery Mascarpone or similar brand
- 6 1/2-inch/1 cm-thick slices bioche or challah bread
- 2 tbsp. salted Irish butter
- mixed berries for serving
- confectioners' sugar for dusting

1. In a medium bowl, whisk together the egg, milk, cinnamon, vanilla, and sugar. Set aside.
2. Spread mascarpone on one side of four of the bread slices. Place a plain slice between the two with cheese to form a sandwich, and then cut the sandwich in half diagonally. Place the stuffed bread into the egg mixture, turn to coat both sides, and let sit for a few minutes until the egg mixture is absorbed.
3. In a large skillet over medium heat, melt the butter. Add the bread and cook for 3–5 minutes on each side or until browned.
4. Serve with a spoonful of mixed berries and dust with confectioners' sugar.

TRADITIONAL FRUIT SCONES

A good scone has always been the cornerstone of traditional Irish baking. It's safe to say, though, that there are as many variations of scone recipes as there are Irish cooks. This one, from a baker friend in Killarney, can be used for plain scones, or you can add sultanas (golden raisins), currants, dried fruit, or your favorite spice, such as Mixed Spice (page 33).

- 3 cups/350 g all-purpose flour
- 3 tbsp. granulated sugar
- 1 tsp. baking soda
- pinch of salt
- 6 tbsp. unsalted Irish butter, cut into pieces
- 1/2 cup/60 g sultanas (golden raisins)
- 1 large egg, beaten
- 3/4 cup/175 ml buttermilk, plus more if needed
- milk for brushing
- softened butter and jam for serving

1. Preheat the oven to 425°F/220°C. Line a baking sheet with parchment paper.
2. Combine the flour, sugar, and salt in a large bowl. Add the butter and, with your fingers or a pastry cutter, cut or work in the butter until the mixture resembles coarse crumbs. Stir in the sultanas.
3. Add the egg and buttermilk, plus more if needed, to form soft dough. Turn the dough out onto a lightly floured surface and pat into a 3/4-inch/2-cm thick round. With a 2 1/2 inch/6 cm biscuit cutter, cut out rounds. Gather scraps and repeat with remaining dough.
4. Place scones on the prepared pan and brush lightly with milk. Bake scones for 18–20 minutes or until the tops are browned. Remove from the oven and serve warm with butter and jam.

Photo crourtesy of Mark Hemauer {http://eggtotheapples.wordpress.com}

BACON-CHEDDAR BISCUITS

T HESE savory scone-like biscuits are a delightful addition to any morning meal. Try them with the Spiced Apple Compote (page 33), a great alternative to sweet jams or preserves.

- 3 slices Irish breakfast bacon, chopped
- 2 1/2 cups/300 g all-purpose flour
- 2 tbsp. granulated sugar
- 1 tbsp. baking powder
- 3/4 tsp. cream of tartar
- 1/2 tsp. salt
- 8 tbsp. unsalted Irish butter, cut into pieces
- 1 cup/225 g grated Kerrygold Aged Cheddar cheese
- 2 tbsp. minced fresh herbs, such as parsley, rosemary, and chives
- 1 large egg
- 1 1/4 cups/300 ml buttermilk

1. In a large skillet over medium heat, cook the bacon, turning frequently, for 7–9 minutes or until lightly browned. Set aside.
2. Preheat the oven to 400°F/200°C. Spray the cups of two 12-well muffin pans with nonstick cooking spray.
3. Combine the flour, sugar, baking powder, cream of tartar, and salt in a food processor fitted with a metal blade. Pulse 2–3 times to blend. Add the butter and process for 10–15 seconds or until the mixture resembles coarse crumbs.
4. Add the cheese and herbs and pulse 2–3 times to blend. Add the egg and buttermilk and process for 10–20 seconds or until soft dough forms. Add the bacon.
5. Spoon the batter into the prepared pan and bake for 23–25 minutes or until the biscuits are lightly browned and a skewer inserted into the center comes out clean. Remove from the oven, transfer to a wire rack, and let cool for 10 minutes.

MRS. MCCANN'S OATY BROWN BREAD

Brown soda bread is served throughout the day in Ireland—with an Irish breakfast, with soup or salad for lunch, and as an accompaniment to dinner. Traditionally, the bread is shaped into a round and an "X" is cut into the center. McCann's oatmeal, both quick-cooking and steel-cut, adds to its rough texture and nutty flavor.

- 3 cups/350 g all-purpose flour
- 1 1/2 cups/175 g coarse whole-wheat flour
- 1/2 cup/60 g quick-cooking Irish oatmeal
- 1/2 cup/60 g steel-cut oatmeal
- 2 1/2 tsp. baking soda
- 5 tbsp. brown sugar
- 4 tbsp. unsalted Irish butter, cut into pieces
- 1 1/2 cups/350 ml buttermilk, plus more if needed
- softened butter for serving

1. Preheat the oven to 425°F/220°C. Lightly dust a baking sheet with flour or spray a 9 inch/22 cm loaf pan with nonstick cooking spray.
2. In a large bowl, stir together the dry ingredients. With your fingers or a pastry cutter, work in the butter. Make a well in the center and stir in the buttermilk. Add more, if needed, to form soft dough.
3. Turn the dough onto a lightly floured surface, and with floured hands, knead for about 1 minute. Shape the dough into a ball and put it in the center of the prepared baking sheet.
4. Flatten the dough into a circle about 1 1/2 inches/3.5 cm thick, and with a serrated knife that has been dipped in flour, cut an "X" through the center of the bread (do not cut all the way through).
5. Bake for 30–35 minutes or until a skewer inserted in the center comes out clean and the bread sounds hollow when tapped on the bottom. Remove from the oven and let cool in the pan on a wire rack for 10 minutes.
6. Turn the bread out onto the rack and let cool for about 1 hour to make slicing easier. Serve slices spread with butter. (Freeze leftover bread to make soda breadcrumbs for Brown Bread Ice Cream, page 152).

WEST CORK NUTTY BROWN BREAD

WEST Cork has become increasingly well known as a center for fine food and fine food producers. In the heart of this scenic area, Skibbereen (Irish for *Sciobairan*, "little boat harbor") is a pleasant town with good pubs, great traditional music, a weekly farmers' market, and the charming West Cork Hotel. Established in 1902, this small hotel on the Ilen River is a favorite among locals, who especially love Chef Dean Diplock's soda bread, which he makes with a soda bread "mix" and enhances with a variety of mixed seeds and nuts. It's one of the best I've tasted recently!

- 1 3/4 cups/200 g Odlum's Brown Bread Mix or similar brand
- 1 cup/115 g whole wheat flour
- 1/2 tsp. baking soda
- 1/2 tsp. salt
- 2 tbsp. sesame seeds
- 2 tbsp. poppy seeds
- 2 tbsp. flax seeds
- 2 cups/500 ml buttermilk, plus more if needed
- 3–4 tbsp. pumpkin seeds for topping

1. Preheat the oven to 350°F/180°C. Spray a 9 inch/22 cm loaf pan with nonstick cooking spray.
2. In a large bowl, combine the bread mix, flour, baking soda, salt, and half of the sesame, poppy, and flax seeds. Make a well in the center, stir in the buttermilk, and add more, if needed, to form soft dough.
3. Spoon the batter into the prepared pan and sprinkle with the remaining sesame, poppy, and flax seeds. Press the pumpkin seeds into the top. Reduce the heat to 300°F/150°C and bake for 50–55 minutes or until a skewer inserted into the center comes out clean.
4. Remove from the oven and let cool on a wire rack before cutting into slices. Serve immediately, or cover with plastic wrap when cooled. (Freeze leftover bread to make soda breadcrumbs for Brown Bread Ice Cream, page 152).

SPOTTED DOG

ANOTHER version of soda bread is this sweet one (often called "Irish Bread" in the U.S.) made with white flour, caraway seeds, and raisins. It's also called "Spotted Dog," "Railway Cake," or "Curnie Cake," depending on the area where it's made. This recipe originated in Co. Donegal with Kathleen McGuire and has been passed down through her daughters.

- 3 cups/350 g all-purpose flour
- 2/3 cup/150 g granulated sugar
- 1 tsp. salt
- 1 tbsp. baking powder
- 1 tsp. baking soda
- 1 1/2 cups/175 g raisins, or half raisins and half sultanas (golden raisins)
- 3 tsp. caraway seeds
- 2 large eggs, beaten
- 2 cups/500 ml buttermilk
- 2 tbsp. salted Irish butter, melted
- softened butter for serving

1. Preheat the oven to 350°F/180°C. Grease and flour a 9 inch/22 cm round baking pan.
2. In a large bowl, combine the flour, sugar, salt, baking powder, and baking soda. Stir in the raisins and caraway seeds. Make a well in the center and stir in the eggs, buttermilk, and butter.
3. Transfer the dough to the prepared pan and bake for about 1 hour, or until the top is golden and a skewer inserted into the center comes out clean. Cool in pan on wire rack for 5 minutes and then invert the bread onto the rack and let cool completely before slicing. Serve slices spread with butter.

LIL AND KITTY'S TEA BRACK

PERFECT for brunch or afternoon tea, the recipe for this fruity brack (the name is derived from the Irish word breac, meaning "speckled") has been handed down three generations (from Lil and Kitty) to Sile Gorman, proprietor with her husband, Vincent, of Gorman's Clifftop House and Restaurant. Basically a light fruit cake, the raisins and sultanas are soaked in tea and sugar overnight to plump them up. Gorman's, located near the small fishing village of Ballydavid on the Dingle Peninsula, Co. Kerry, is a member of Good Food Ireland.

- 1 1/2 cups/175 g raisins
- 1 1/2 cups/175 g sultanas (golden raisins)
- generous 1/2 cup/115 g (packed) brown sugar
- 1 cup/250 ml cold tea
- 4 tbsp. unsalted Irish butter, melted
- 1 large egg, beaten
- 4 tbsp. chopped dried cranberries
- 4 tbsp. mixed peel
- 4 tbsp. chopped almonds
- 2 1/4 cups/300 g all-purpose flour
- 1 heaping tsp. baking powder

1. In a large bowl, combine the raisins, sultanas, brown sugar, and tea. Cover and let soak overnight.
2. Preheat the oven to 350°F/180°C. Spray a 9 inch/22 cm loaf pan with nonstick cooking spray.
3. Stir the butter into the fruit mixture, and then stir in the egg, cranberries, mixed peel, and almonds. Sift together the flour and baking powder and stir into the fruit mixture. Spoon into the prepared pan and bake for 55–60 minutes or until the top is golden and a skewer inserted into the center comes out clean.
4. Remove from the oven. Transfer to a wire rack and let cool in pan for 15 minutes. Invert loaf onto rack and let cool completely before slicing.

LOUGH ESKE CASTLE BLUEBERRY-WHITE CHOCOLATE MUFFINS

AMERICAN-STYLE muffins are showing up more and more in café and coffeehouse menus and on breakfast buffets in country houses and hotels throughout Ireland. These, from Chef Philipp Ferber of Lough Eske Castle Hotel, Donegal Town, get their light texture from buttermilk and their added flavor from white chocolate and lemon zest.

- 2 cups/225 g all-purpose flour
- 3/4 tsp. baking powder
- 1/2 tsp. baking soda
- 1/4 tsp. salt
- 3/4 cup/175 g granulated sugar
- 2 large eggs
- 4 tbsp. salted Irish butter, melted
- 1 1/2 cups/350 ml buttermilk
- 4 oz./115 g white chocolate, melted
- 1 tsp. lemon zest
- 1 1/2 cups/225 g blueberries
- softened butter for serving

1. Preheat the oven to 400°F/20°C. Spray a 12-well muffin pan with non-stick cooking spray.
2. In a large bowl, combine the flour, baking powder, baking soda, salt, and sugar. Set aside.
3. In another large bowl, whisk together the eggs, butter, and buttermilk until smooth. Stir in the flour mixture and then stir in the white chocolate, lemon zest, and blueberries.
4. Divide the batter into the prepared pan and bake for 20–23 minutes. Remove from the oven and let cool on a wire rack for 10–15 minutes.

CHAPTER No. 2

STARTERS, SOUPS, SALADS

The food of the farmers is plain, wholesome and substantial, consisting of fried bacon or hung beef, boiled beef (chiefly in broth). Excellent broth made of beef, groats and oatmeal, leeks and cabbage is a favorite and comfortable dish.

JAMES BOYLE
Ordnance Survey Memoirs, 1838

ARLINGTON LODGE CHICKEN LIVER PÂTÉ WITH RED ONION MARMALADE

Pâtés are popular fare in Irish pubs and restaurants, and they're often served with piquant sauces and relishes. This classic dish is a favorite at Maurice Keller's Arlington Lodge, a stately Georgian mansion built in 1760 in the lovely maritime city of Waterford. Mr. Keller recommends serving it with any tangy relish or chutney, but I love it with sweet-savory Red Onion Marmalade, a spread that you can also use with meats, poultry, and cheese. Arlington Lodge is a member of Good Food Ireland.

- 8 slices Irish breakfast bacon, chopped
- 1 large onion, coarsely chopped
- 4 cloves garlic, minced
- 2 lb./900 kg chicken livers, membranes removed
- 12 tbsp. salted Irish butter
- salt and freshly ground black pepper
- 1/2 bunch fresh flat-leaf parsley, chopped, plus additional for garnish
- Melba toast or buttered toast for serving

1. In a large skillet over medium heat, cook the bacon, turning frequently, for 7–9 minutes or until lightly browned. Add the onion and garlic to the skillet, reduce heat to medium-low, and cook for 8–10 minutes or until soft and lightly browned.
2. Add the chicken livers and cook for another 8–10 minutes or until nearly cooked through but still slightly pink inside.
3. As the livers cook, add the butter a few tbsp. at a time and stir to incorporate. Season with salt and pepper, and then stir in the parsley. Let cool for about 5 minutes. Transfer the mixture to a food processor and pulse 3–4 times or until coarsely chopped.
4. Line a terrine or pâté dish with plastic wrap, leaving a 2 inch/5 cm overhang on all sides. Spoon in the chicken liver mixture, cover with the plastic wrap, and refrigerate until the butter solidifies (can be stored for up to 5 days).
5. To serve, unwrap the terrine and invert onto a serving plate. Sprinkle with additional parsley and then cut into slices and serve with the marmalade and toast.

RED ONION MARMALADE

- 2 large red onions, chopped
- 1 cup/225 g (packed) dark brown sugar
- 1 cup/250 ml red wine vinegar
- 1/4 tsp. fresh thyme
- 1 tbsp. minced garlic

1. In a medium saucepan over medium heat, combine the onions, brown sugar, vinegar, thyme, and garlic. Bring to a boil and then reduce the heat to simmer.
2. Cook, stirring frequently, for 40–45 minutes, uncovered, or until the liquid is nearly evaporated. Stir in the thyme, remove from the heat, and let cool completely. Cover and refrigerate for up to 2 weeks.

Makes about 1 1/2 cups/350 ml

SMOKED SALMON WITH TANGY HORSERADISH SAUCE

SMOKED Irish salmon acquires its inimitable dark orange color and subtle flavor from the traditional method of smoking over an open wood fire or in a kiln. It can be smoked horizontally on trays or suspended over an oak or beech wood fire. There are countless smokehouses in Ireland where salmon is smoked using both methods, but the flavor and texture is determined by the quality of the fish, whether wild, organic, or conventionally farmed. Regardless of the smoking method or the origin of the fish, most agree that smoked salmon is best served as simply as possible, perhaps with a slice of brown soda bread and this tangy sauce.

1. In a small bowl, whisk together the mayonnaise, parsley, horseradish, mustard, lemon juice, and pepper.
2. Place 2 slices of soda bread on each of 6 plates and top each with 1 slice of salmon. Spoon the sauce over the top and garnish with dill.

HORSERADISH SAUCE

- 5 tbsp. mayonnaise
- 1 tbsp. chopped fresh flat-leaf parsley
- 1 tbsp. prepared horseradish
- 1 tbsp. Lakeshore Wholegrain Mustard or similar brand
- 1 tsp. fresh lemon juice
- 1/4 tsp. freshly ground black pepper
- 12 slices Brown Soda Bread (page 41)
- 12 slices smoked salmon
- fresh dill sprigs for garnish

BERE ISLAND SCALLOPS WITH POTATO PURÉE AND SWEET ONION RELISH

SCALLOPS from the waters near Bere Island, located off the southwest coast of Ireland in Bantry Bay, Co. Cork, are prized for their sweet flavor. At Lough Eske Castle, Donegal's only five-star hotel, Chef Philipp Ferber rests them on a bed of potato purée and tops them with cashews, bacon bits, and chives. The sweet onion relish provides a little kick.

SCALLOPS

- 2 slices Irish bacon, chopped
- 2 tbsp. olive oil
- 12 large scallops, rinsed and patted dry
- salt and freshly ground pepper to taste
- 4 tbsp. toasted and crushed cashews
- 1 tsp. minced fresh chives
- 1 tsp. smoked paprika powder

1. In a large skillet over medium heat, cook the bacon until browned. Remove from pan and reserve.
2. In the same skillet over medium-high heat, heat the oil. Cook the scallops for about 3 minutes on each side or until browned. Season with salt and pepper.
3. To serve, divide the potato purée into 4 shallow soup bowls. Put a tbsp. of the sweet onion relish in the center and 3 scallops around it. Sprinkle with the bacon, cashews, chives, and paprika.

SWEET ONION RELISH

- 4 tbsp. granulated sugar
- 1/2 cup/125 ml white wine vinegar, plus more if needed
- 3 large onions, chopped
- 1 (8 oz./225 g) package salted Irish butter
- 1 cup/250 ml homemade vegetable stock or canned low-salt vegetable broth
- 1 bay leaf
- salt and freshly ground pepper to taste

1. In a medium saucepan over medium heat, cook the sugar, stirring constantly, for 3–5 minutes or until caramelized. Add the vinegar and deglaze the pan. Stir in the onions, butter, stock, bay leaf, salt, and pepper. Cook for about 20 minutes or until the onions are very soft. Remove from the heat, and with an immersion blender or hand mixer, blend until smooth. Season with salt and pepper.

Makes about 3 cups

POTATO PÚREE

- 2 large boiling potatoes, peeled and cut into 1 1/2 inch/3.5 cm pieces
- 4 tbsp. unsalted Irish butter
- 1/4 cup/60 ml heavy (whipping) cream, plus more if needed
- salt and freshly ground pepper to taste

1. Cook the potatoes in salted boiling water for about 15 minutes or until tender. Drain and mash. Stir in the butter and cream. (The mixture should be slightly thicker than soup, so add more cream if needed.) Season with salt and pepper.

Photo courtesy of Fermanagh Black Bacon Cookbook

OYSTERS WITH GARLIC-HERB BREADCRUMBS

L IKE smoked salmon, Irish oysters are considered food "fit for the gods." It's hard to believe the prized mollusk was once considered "famine food" and associated with poverty and hard times. Carried in panniers by donkeys along dirt-track roads, the seaweed-wrapped shellfish were sold not by the dozen but by the barrelful and were often given away free by Dublin publicans and innkeepers. Native wild oysters are still synonymous with Galway Bay, where they fatten in its clear and clean water, but you'll find them throughout the country—offered straight from the shell with a squeeze of lemon, topped with tangy mignonette sauce, broiled with bacon and watercress (see Variation), or with these garlic-herb breadcrumbs.

- ○ 3 tbsp. Kerrygold Garlic and Herb butter
- ○ 1 tsp. fresh lemon juice
- ○ 1 cup/115 g fresh white breadcrumbs
- ○ salt and freshly ground pepper to taste
- ○ 24 shucked oysters
- ○ 1 tbsp. minced fresh flat-leaf parsley
- ○ lemon wedges for serving

1. Preheat the broiler. In a large skillet over medium heat, melt the butter. Remove from the heat and stir in the lemon juice, breadcrumbs, salt, and pepper.
2. Place the oysters on a broiler pan and divide the breadcrumbs mixture evenly over the oysters. Broil 4–5 inches from the heat source for about 3 minutes or until the breadcrumbs are lightly browned.
3. To serve, place 4 oysters on each of 6 plates, sprinkle with the parsley, and garnish with a lemon wedge.

VARIATION: GRILLED OYSTERS WITH BLACK BACON AND WATERCRESS

E NNISKILLEN butcher Pat O'Doherty, famous for his Fermanagh Black Bacon, adds bacon, watercress, and spinach to his recipe for grilled (broiled) oysters. The recipe is adapted from his *Fermanagh Black Bacon Cookbook.*

1. Melt 3 tbsp. butter. Stir in 4 tbsp. each chopped watercress and chopped spinach, 3 tbsp. chopped scallions, 1 tbsp. minced fresh flat-leaf parsley, 2 tsp. chopped celery, 1 tsp. fresh white breadcrumbs, 1 tsp. Pernod, pinch of cayenne, salt, and freshly ground pepper to taste.
2. Transfer the mixture to a small bowl and chill for about 1 hour.
3. In a large skillet over medium heat, cook 4 slices of bacon, chopped, for 7–9 minutes or until browned. Stir into the watercress mixture.
4. Preheat the broiler. Place 24 shucked oysters on a broiler pan and divide the watercress mixture evenly over the oysters. Sprinkle with 2 more tsp. of breadcrumbs.
5. Broil 4–5 inches from the heat source for about 3 minutes or until the breadcrumbs are lightly browned. To serve, place 4 oysters on each of 6 plates, sprinkle with the parsley, and garnish with a lemon wedge.

Photo courtesy of Guinness Storehouse

MUSSELS WITH GUINNESS

STEAMED mussels are an easy-to-prepare and easy-on-the-budget meal. Steaming in white wine is the classic method, but once you've tasted them paired with Guinness and a touch of dill, you'll never go back to wine. This version, adapted from a recipe served at The Brewery Bar at The Guinness Storehouse, Dublin's number-one visitor attraction, can be on the table in under 20 minutes. The Brewery Bar is a member of Good Food Ireland.

- 4 tbsp. salted Irish butter
- 2 large onions, chopped
- 1 (1 1/2 oz.) bottle Guinness draught
- 6 lb./3 kg mussels, scrubbed and debearded
- salt and freshly ground pepper to taste
- 2 cups/500 ml cream
- 2 tbsp. chopped fresh flat-leaf parsley
- 1 tbsp. chopped fresh dill

1. In a large pot over medium heat, melt the butter. Add the onions and cook for 2–3 minutes or until soft but not browned. Add the Guinness, mussels, salt, and pepper. Bring to a boil and then cover and cook, stirring once or twice, for 6–8 minutes or until the mussels begin to open.
2. Add the cream, 1 tbsp. of the parsley, and the dill. Return gently to boil and cook 2–3 minutes longer or until all the mussels open (discard any that don't open.)
3. To serve, ladle the mussels into shallow bowls and sprinkle with the remaining tbsp. of parsley.

MRS. O'SULLIVAN'S MARKET PLATE WITH PEAR-DRIED CRANBERRY CHUTNEY

JOHN O'Sullivan, who operates a dairy farm near Clonakilty, Co. Cork, produces milk for the Kerrygold cooperative from his herd of 50 cows. To celebrate St. Patrick's Day, he and his family head to the local parade and then return home to enjoy this lovely market plate of meats, fish, and Irish cheese, some of which might be made from his own milk. Mrs. O'Sullivan assembles it and offers it with assorted breads and her homemade Pear-Dried Cranberry Chutney.

- 8 slices Kerrygold Dubliner cheese
- 8 slices Kerrygold Reserve Cheddar cheese
- 8 slices Kerrygold Blarney Castle cheese
- 8 slices smoked ham
- 8 slices roast beef
- 8 slices smoked duck or chicken breast
- 8 oz./225 g smoked trout
- 8 slices smoked salmon, preferably Irish
- roasted peppers for serving
- Lakeshore Wholegrain Mustard or similar brand for serving
- sliced cucumber for serving
- Brown Soda Bread (page 41) for serving
- olive oil for drizzling (optional)

1. On a large decorative platter, arrange the cheeses, meats, poultry, and fish.
2. Arrange the roasted peppers and cucumbers, and serve with the mustard, chutney, and bread. Drizzle the meats and cheese with olive oil, if desired.

PEAR-DRIED CRANBERRY CHUTNEY

- 1 tbsp. canola oil
- 1 medium onion, chopped
- 3 firm ripe pears, peeled, cored, and chopped
- 3/4 cup/90 g dried cranberries
- 1/2 cup/115 g (packed) light brown sugar
- 4 tbsp. cider vinegar
- 1 tbsp. grated fresh ginger
- 1/2 tsp. ground cinnamon
- 1/4 tsp. ground cloves
- pinch of cayenne pepper

1. In medium saucepan over medium heat, heat the oil. Add the onion and cook, stirring frequently, for 3–5 minutes or until soft but not browned. Add the pears, cranberries, brown sugar, vinegar, ginger, cinnamon, cloves, and pepper.
2. Bring to a boil and then reduce heat and simmer, stirring frequently, for about 30 minutes or until pears are soft and most of the liquid has evaporated.
3. Remove from the heat and let cool completely. Cover and refrigerate for up to 1 month. Serve the chutney at room temperature with the meat and cheese.

Makes about 2 1/2 cups

AMERICAN WHITE WINE

Photo courtesy of Good Food Ireland

Serves 8

GLEESON'S GOAT CHEESE TERRINE WITH ROCKET SALAD

MARY and Eamonn Gleeson have operated their eponymous townhouse and restaurant on Market Square, Roscommon Town, for more than 15 years. To round out their commitment to good food and good eating, they've also added a gourmet deli and artisan food and wine shop. This easy-to-assemble goat cheese terrine is one of their most popular starters, but it would also make a delicious picnic dish. Serve it with tangy rocket (arugula) salad, a few toasted pine nuts, and a drizzle of avocado or olive oil. Gleeson's is a member of Good Food Ireland.

- 2 tbsp. olive oil
- 1 small courgette (zucchini), diced
- 1 yellow pepper, seeded and diced
- 1 small red onion, diced
- 1 fennel bulb, diced
- 4–5 fresh basil leaves
- salt and freshly ground pepper
- juice and grated zest of 1 lemon
- 1 lb./450 g goat cheese, preferably Irish
- 2 tbsp. cream cheese
- 10 oz./300 g rocket
- 1/2 cup/60 g pine nuts, toasted
- avocado or olive oil for drizzling

1. In a large skillet over medium heat, heat the olive oil. Add the courgette, pepper, onion, and fennel and cook for 3–5 minutes or until the vegetables are tender but still crisp. Season with salt and pepper and stir in the lemon juice and rind. Sprinkle with the basil. Remove from the heat.
2. Combine the goat cheese and cream cheese in a food processor and process for 10–15 seconds or until blended and smooth. Line a terrine or pâté dish with plastic wrap, leaving a 2 inch/5 cm overhang on all sides. With a piping bag or spatula, put 1/3 of the cheese mixture into the dish and smooth with a spatula.
3. Top with half of the vegetables and then repeat with another third of the cheese, the remaining half of the vegetables, and finish with the remaining cheese, smoothing each layer. Fold the plastic wrap over the top of the dish and refrigerate the terrine for at least 3 hours and up to 1 day.
4. To serve, unwrap the terrine, invert onto a serving plate, and cut into slices. Serve with the rocket, sprinkle with the pine nuts, and drizzle with the avocado or olive oil.

Serves 6

BALLYVOLANE CHEESE SOUFFLÉ

ONE of Ireland's premier country house hotels, Ballyvolane, Castleyon, Co. Cork, is also well known for its salmon fishery on the Blackwater River. The classical Georgian home was built in 1728 for a once Lord Chief Justice of Ireland but has been thoroughly modernized over the centuries to become one of North Cork's most favorite getaways. Now in the hands of Justin and Jenny Green, who source ingredients from their own walled garden and also from local artisans, farmers, and butchers, dining here is a genuine country house experience. You might be offered this lovely starter made with Dubliner cheese, a dish that can be served immediately or reheated using the "twice-baked" technique (see Note). Ballyvolane is a member of Good Food Ireland.

- 3 tbsp. salted Irish butter, plus more for greasing ramekins
- 1 1/4 cups/300 ml milk
- pinch of ground nutmeg
- 4 tbsp. all-purpose flour
- 1/4 tsp. salt
- pinch of dry mustard
- pinch of cayenne pepper
- 3/4 cup/90 g grated Dubliner cheese
- 3 large eggs, separated
- mixed salad for garnish
- balsamic syrup or glaze for drizzling (optional)

NOTE: For "twice-baked" soufflés, prepare as above and then cool on wire rack. Run a small knife along edges to loosen soufflés and then invert them onto an ovenproof dish. Preheat the oven to 425°F/220°C. Sprinkle about 2 tsp. shredded Dubliner cheese over each soufflé. Season 3/4 cup/175 ml heavy (whipping) cream with salt and pepper. Pour it over each soufflé and cover completely. Cook for about 10 minutes or until the tops are golden and heated through. With a metal spatula, transfer soufflés to salad plates and serve as above.

1. Preheat the oven to 400°F/200°C. Generously butter six 6 oz. ramekins.
2. In a large heatproof bowl, microwave milk and nutmeg on high for about 1 1/2 minutes or until hot.
3. In medium saucepan over medium-low heat, melt the butter. Whisk in the flour, salt, mustard, and cayenne. Cook for 1 minute, and then gradually add the hot milk, whisking until smooth. Simmer for 3 minutes, whisking frequently. Remove from the heat and stir in cheese until melted. Whisk in the egg yolks until blended.
4. In a medium bowl, beat the egg whites with an electric mixer on high until stiff but not dry. Stir one quarter of the egg whites into the cheese mixture to lighten. Gently fold in the remaining whites and spoon the mixture into the prepared dishes.
5. Place the dishes into a large baking pan and add enough hot water to come halfway up the side of the dishes. Bake for 18–20 minutes or until the center is puffed and set.
6. To serve, place a ramekin on each of 6 salad plates. Arrange some salad greens on each and drizzle with balsamic syrup, if using.

Serves 4–6

DUNGUAIRE CASTLE LEEK AND POTATO SOUP

DUNGUAIRE is a small seventeenth century castle situated just outside the picturesque village of Kinvara on the shores of Galway Bay. One of three castles where the famous medieval banquets take place, Dunguaire is well known for the performance that celebrates the works of Irish literary giants such as Synge, Yeats, Shaw, and O'Casey. A four-course meal is served during the entertainment, including this leek and potato soup, also known as *brotchán foltchep* (from the Irish words meaning "broth" and "leeks"). Today, most cooks thicken the leek broth with potatoes instead of oatmeal, the traditional thickener, and the soup can be switched from homespun to modern by swirling tangy buttermilk or whipped cream into it, topping it with a dollop of crème frâiche, or adding spices. Shannon Heritage operates the Dunguaire Castle Banquet from April to October.

- 4 tbsp. unsalted Irish butter
- 1 medium onion, chopped
- 1 large leek (white and light green parts only), sliced
- 4 medium boiling potatoes, peeled and cut into 1 1/2 inch/3.5 cm pieces
- 1/2 tsp. fresh thyme
- 4 cups/1 L homemade chicken stock or canned low-salt chicken broth
- chopped fresh flat-leaf parsley
- salt and freshly ground white pepper to taste
- crème fraîche for topping

1. In a large saucepan over medium heat, melt the butter. Add the onion, leeks, and potatoes. Stir to coat them with the butter and cook, stirring frequently, for 5–7 minutes or until soft but not browned. Add the parsley and thyme.
2. Add the stock or broth, bring to a boil, and then reduce heat to low, cover, and simmer for 20–25 minutes or until the vegetables are tender. Remove from heat and let the soup cool for 10–15 minutes.
3. Working in batches, transfer to a food processor or blender and process until smooth. Return the purée to the saucepan over medium heat and season with salt and pepper. Add some of the parsley and simmer until heated through.
4. To serve, ladle the soup into shallow bowls, swirl 1 tbsp. crème fraîche into each serving, and sprinkle with more parsley.

CAULIFLOWER SOUP WITH JULIENNE OF SMOKED SALMON

I've enjoyed cauliflower soup in Ireland on many occasions, and it's never been served the same way twice. A chef friend of mine suggested that the soup is like a blank culinary canvas to which almost any other flavor can be added—garlic, cheese, potatoes, carrots, sour cream, or smoked salmon—as in this delicious version from Mark Johnston, Executive Chef at the luxurious Park Hotel Kenmare, Co. Kerry. Founded in 1897, The Park is set in a heavenly location overlooking Kenmare Bay in the heart of Ireland's most scenic countryside. The Park Kenmare is a member of Good Food Ireland.

- 1 tbsp. olive oil
- 2 tbsp. salted Irish butter
- 1 medium onion, finely chopped
- 4 small leeks (white part only), sliced
- salt and freshly ground pepper to taste
- 1 large head cauliflower, cut into florets
- 1 boiling potato, peeled and sliced
- 4 cups/1 L homemade chicken stock or canned low-salt chicken broth
- 2/3 cup/150 ml heavy (whipping) cream
- 1/4 tsp. ground nutmeg
- 2–3 slices smoked salmon, cut into thin strips
- chopped fresh dill for garnish

1. In a large saucepan over medium heat, heat the oil and butter. Add the onion and leeks, season with salt and pepper, and cook for 8–10 minutes or until the vegetables are soft but not browned.
2. Add the cauliflower, potato, and stock. Bring to a boil and then reduce heat and simmer for 30–40 minutes, covered, or until the cauliflower is tender. Remove from heat and let the soup cool for 10–15 minutes.
3. Working in batches, transfer to a food processor or blender and process until smooth. Return the purée to the saucepan over medium heat and stir in the cream and nutmeg. Season with salt and pepper.
4. To serve, ladle the soup into shallow bowls, garnish with salmon, and sprinkle with dill.

Photo courtesy of Ashford Castle

CREAM OF SMOKED GUBBEEN SOUP WITH OATMEAL-FRIED PARSLEY BISCUITS

ASHFORD Castle, in Cong, Co. Mayo, is one of Ireland's earliest stately hotels. The original castle dates from the thirteenth century and was once the estate of the Guinness family. Executive Chef Stefan Matz oversees four unique dining experiences at Ashford, ranging from the elegant George V dining room to casual Cullen's, a thatched cottage on the property that overlooks Lough Cong. Chef Matz enjoys a reputation for his inspired use of seasonal ingredients and his unique mix of flavors and textures. In this recipe, he combines the sharpness of Kerrygold's Dubliner cheese with the beech- and oak-smoked flavors of Gubbeen, a farmhouse cheese made in Schull, Co. Cork. His fried parsley biscuits are a bonus!

- 4 tbsp. salted Irish butter
- 1 large onion, chopped
- 1/2 small leek (white part only), chopped
- 2 boiling potatoes, peeled and cut into 1 1/2 inch/3.5 cm pieces
- 1/3 cup/75 ml white cooking wine
- 5 cups/1.5 L water
- 1 vegetable bouillon cube
- 1/2 cup/60 g grated Dubliner cheese
- 1/2 cup/125 ml heavy (whipping) cream
- 1/2 cup/60 g grated Smoked Gubbeen cheese
- salt and freshly ground pepper to taste

1. In a large saucepan over medium heat, melt the butter. Stir in the onion and leek and cook for 3–5 minutes or until soft but not browned. Add the potato and cook for 2–3 minutes longer. Add the wine and cook for about 5 minutes or until the wine evaporates.
2. Add the water and bouillon cube, bring to a boil, and cook, stirring frequently, for 5–8 minutes or until the cube dissolves. Add the Dubliner, reduce the heat, and simmer, stirring occasionally, for 18–20 minutes or until the cheese is blended and the potatoes are tender. Remove the soup from the heat and let cool for about 10 minutes.
3. Working in batches, transfer to a food processor or blender and process until smooth. Return the purée to the saucepan over medium heat and stir in the cream and Gubbeen. Simmer until heated through. Season with salt and pepper.
4. To serve, ladle the soup into shallow bowls and serve with the biscuits.

CONTINUED ON NEXT PAGE

OATMEAL-FRIED PARSLEY BISCUITS

- 2 tbsp. canola oil
- handful fresh flat-leaf parsley, stems removed
- 8 tbsp. salted Irish butter, at room temperature
- 1 tbsp. sugar
- 1 cup/115 g all-purpose flour
- 1 cup/115 g McCann's Irish oatmeal
- 1 tbsp. baking powder
- pinch of salt
- 2 large egg yolks
- 1/2 tsp. lemon pepper

1. Preheat the oven to 350°F/180°C. Line a baking sheet with parchment paper.
2. In a small skillet over medium-high heat, heat the oil. Fry the parsley for 1–2 minutes or until crisp. With a slotted spoon, transfer to paper towels to drain. Crumble and reserve.
3. In a large bowl, cream the butter and sugar with an electric mixer on medium until smooth.
4. In another large bowl, whisk together the flour, oatmeal, baking powder, and salt. Stir the dry ingredients into the butter mixture and then stir in the egg yolks, lemon pepper, and fried parsley. Gently knead the mixture and form into a disk.
5. On a lightly floured surface, roll out the dough to a 1/2-inch/1-cm thick square. Cut the dough into 1-inch/2.5-cm wide strips and then cut the strips into twenty 2-inch/5-cm long biscuits. Bake for 10 minutes and then turn each biscuit over and bake for 3–4 minutes longer or until lightly browned.
6. 6. Remove from the oven and let the biscuits cool in the pan on a wire rack. (Can be stored in an airtight container for up to 2 days).

Makes 20 biscuits

Photo courtesy of Shannon Heritage

ADARE MANOR ROASTED VEGETABLE SOUP WITH HERBED CREAM

NEO-GOTHIC Adare Manor, located in the thatched village of Adare, Co. Limerick, is one of the most stunning hotels in Ireland. It was the family seat of the Dunravens from the middle of the nineteenth century until 1982. Now in the capable hands of the Kane family, the hotel retains its original grandeur but is nicely complemented by a championship golf course and stunning golf villas. For dining choices, guests can enjoy elegant fare like this indulgent soup from Executive Chef Mark O'Donoghue in the Manor's Oakroom, or in its bistro-style Carriagehouse.

- 2 carrots, diced
- 2 parsnips, diced
- 1 medium sweet potato, peeled and diced
- 1 celeriac (celery root), peeled and diced
- 1 small turnip, peeled and diced
- 6 tbsp. olive oil
- 4 tbsp. salted Irish butter
- 1 medium onion, chopped
- 1/2 leek (white part only), diced
- 2 stalks celery, chopped
- 4 cloves garlic, minced
- 1 sprig thyme
- 1 sprig rosemary
- 6 cups/1 1/2 L homemade vegetable stock or canned low-salt vegetable broth
- salt and freshly ground pepper to taste
- 2/3 cup/150 ml heavy (whipping) cream
- 2 tbsp. minced fresh herbs, such as parsley, chervil, and chives

1. Preheat the oven to 425°F/220°C.
2. In a large ovenproof dish, combine the carrots, parsnips, sweet potato, celeriac, and turnip. Toss to coat with the olive oil, and roast, stirring once or twice, for 18–20 minutes or until the vegetables are lightly browned.
3. In a large saucepan over medium heat, melt the butter. Add the onion, leek, celery, garlic, thyme, and rosemary, and cook, stirring frequently, for 6–8 minutes or until the vegetables are soft but not browned.
4. Add the roasted vegetables and stock or broth to the saucepan, bring to a boil, and then reduce the heat and simmer for 20–25 minutes or until the vegetables are tender. Remove from the heat and let cool for 10 minutes. Remove thyme and rosemary sprigs and discard.
5. Working in batches, transfer the mixture to a food processor or blender and purée until smooth. Return to the saucepan and simmer until heated through. Season with salt and pepper.
6. In a medium bowl, whip the cream with an electric mixer on high until soft peaks form. Fold in the herbs.
7. To serve, ladle the soup into shallow bowls and put a spoonful of the herbed-cream on top.

BRICIN SEAFOOD CHOWDER

EVERY region of Ireland has its own version of this chowder, a creamy soup that showcases the best of native fish and shellfish. The word *chowder* is an anglicized version of *chaudière*, the French word for the large iron cauldron in which fishermen used to make their soups. This recipe, from Johnny and Paddy Maguire's Bricín, a restaurant and craft shop in the heart of Killarney (20 High Street), Co. Kerry, also includes mushrooms and tomato. Serve this with Brown Soda Bread (page 41).

- 10 tbsp. unsalted Irish butter
- 1 medium onion, chopped
- 1 clove garlic, minced
- 1 carrot, grated
- 8 white mushrooms, finely chopped
- 1/2 cup/60 g all-purpose flour
- 4 cups/1 L milk
- 2 cups/500 ml homemade fish stock or bottled clam juice, plus more for thinning
- 3/4 cup/175 ml dry white wine
- 1/4 lb./115 g mussels, steamed, shells discarded
- 1/4 lb./115 g clams, steamed, shells discarded
- 1/2 lb./225 g mixed seafood, such as salmon, shrimp, and scallops
- 1 large tomato, diced
- 2 tbsp. chopped fennel fronds
- salt and freshly ground pepper to taste
- 1 tbsp. minced fresh herbs, such as parsley, chervil, and chives (optional)

1. In a large skillet over medium heat, melt 2 tbsp. of the butter. Add the onion, garlic, carrot, and mushrooms, and cook, stirring constantly, for 3–4 minutes or until the vegetables are soft but not browned. Set aside.
2. In a large saucepan over medium heat, melt the remaining 8 tbsp. of the butter. Stir in the flour and cook for 1–2 minutes or until smooth. Slowly add the milk and cook, whisking constantly, for 3–5 minutes or until the mixture is smooth.
3. Add the fish stock or clam juice and wine, bring slowly to a boil, and cook for 4–5 minutes or until the mixture thickens. Stir in the shellfish and seafood and then stir in the vegetables, tomato, and fennel. Season with salt and pepper, and cook for 5–8 minutes longer or until the fish is cooked and the chowder is heated through. Thin with additional stock or clam juice, if desired.
4. To serve, ladle chowder into shallow bowls and sprinkle with the herbs, if using.

GRILLED PEARS, ROCKET, AND CASHEL BLUE SALAD

A griddle pan is one of those essential pieces of kitchen equipment that one usually thinks of for grilling meats and vegetables. Use it here for warming and coloring ripe pears to mix with peppery rocket (arugula), salty prosciutto, and buttery Cashel Blue, Ireland's original farmhouse blue from Beechmount Farm, Co. Tipperary. Top with Candied Pecans (page 173), if desired. A great substitute for prosciutto is air-dried pork, lamb, or beef from Connemara craft butcher James McGeough. Cashel Blue Farmhouse Cheese and McGeough Butchers are members of Good Food Ireland.

- 4 firm, ripe pears
- 4 tbsp. olive oil
- freshly ground pepper to taste
- 1 (4 oz./100 g) bag of rocket
- 1 tbsp. balsamic vinegar
- 8 slices prosciutto
- 4 oz./115 g crumbled Cashel Blue cheese

1. Cut the pears in half, core, and cut each half into 3 slices. Brush the slices with 2 tbsp. of the olive oil and sprinkle with the pepper.
2. Heat a grill pan until very hot, add the pears, and cook for 2–3 minutes on each side or until lightly browned with grill marks. Set aside.
3. In a large bowl, toss the rocket with the remaining 2 tbsp. of olive oil and the vinegar.
4. To serve, arrange the rocket on 4 salad plates and top with the grilled pears, 2 slices of prosciutto, and the blue cheese. Sprinkle with additional ground pepper and pecans, if using.

BACON, BIBB, AND APPLE SALAD WITH DUHALLOW DRESSING

BIBB lettuce (also known as butter lettuce), Irish bacon, and chopped apples are the basis for this refreshing salad. It's topped with a creamy dressing made with Duhallow, a semi-soft cheese crafted by Mary Burns in Kanturk, Co. Cork, from pasteurized milk from her herd of pedigreed Friesian cows. The cheese develops its unique flavor from the flora that has built up in the maturing rooms, where the wheels are allowed to sit and breathe as they age naturally. Mrs. Burns also makes the well-known Ardrahan cheese, similar in flavor but with a washed rind. Ardrahan Farmhouse Cheese is a member of Good Food Ireland.

- 4 slices Irish bacon, chopped
- 3 tbsp. olive oil
- 1 large cooking apple, cored and chopped
- salt and freshly ground pepper to taste
- 2 small heads of Bibb lettuce, torn into pieces
- 1 tbsp. fresh lemon juice

1. In a large skillet over medium heat, cook the bacon, turning frequently, for 7–9 minutes or until lightly browned. Add 1 tbsp. of the olive oil and the apples. Sauté for 3–5 minutes or until slightly tender. Season with salt and pepper.
2. Arrange the lettuce on 4 salad plates and drizzle with the remaining 2 tbsp. of olive oil and the lemon juice.
3. To serve, divide the warm apples and bacon over the lettuce, and spoon the dressing on top.

DUHALLOW CHEESE DRESSING

- 2/3 cup/150 ml sour cream
- 1 tbsp. apple cider
- 2 oz./60 g Duhallow (or Ardrahan) cheese, rind removed, chopped
- dash of cider vinegar

1. In a small saucepan over medium heat, combine the sour cream, cider, cheese, and vinegar.
2. Cook, whisking gently, for 3–5 minutes or until the cheese has melted and the dressing is smooth and creamy. Let cool.

WARM ST. TOLA GOAT'S CHEESE SALAD WITH BALSAMIC-GLAZED STRAWBERRIES

ST. Tola is a goat's cheese made from raw organic milk from Siobhan Ni Ghairbhith's own herd at Inagh Farmhouse, Ennis, Co. Clare. The cheese is available in fresh and mature versions: the young is brilliant white with a creamy flavor, while mature St. Tola develops a yellowish rind with citrus/herbal notes. For this salad, Executive Chef Mark Johnston of The Park Hotel Kenmare, Co. Kerry, bakes slices of young cheese on toasted brioche and then pairs it with balsamic-glazed strawberries and rocket (arugula) salad. The Park Kenmare is a member of Good Food Ireland.

- 1 1/4 cups/300 ml balsamic vinegar
- 1/2 cup/115 g granulated sugar
- 12 fresh strawberries, halved
- four 1/2-inch/1 cm-thick slices brioche, toasted
- four 1/2-inch/1 cm-thick slices St. Tola goat's cheese
- 4 tbsp. sliced almonds
- 1 small pear, cored and thinly sliced
- one 4 oz./100 g bag of rocket
- olive oil for drizzling
- freshly ground black pepper

1. In a small saucepan over medium heat, combine the vinegar and sugar. Cook, stirring frequently, for 20–30 minutes or until reduced to a syrup consistency (alternately, use prepared balsamic glaze). Let cool. When the glaze is cool, stir in the strawberries.
2. Preheat the oven to 350°F/180°C.
3. Put the toasted brioche on a baking sheet and top with goat's cheese and almonds. Bake for 8–10 minutes or until the cheese is lightly browned.
4. To serve, arrange the rocket on 4 salad plates, toss with the strawberries and pear, and drizzle with olive oil. Place the goat's cheese toast in the center and sprinkle with pepper.

Welcome to:-
LOWRY'S BAR

SOUP
SANDWICHES

TOASTED
SANDWICHES

SMOKED
SALMON

TEA & COFFEE

ESPRESSO
CAPPUCCINO

Chapter
No. 3

STEWS, SAVORY PIES, AND TARTS

The more carrots you chop, the more turnips you slit, the more murphies you peel, the more onions you cry over, the more bullbeef you butch, the more mutton you crackerhack, the more potherbs you pound, the fiercer the fire and the longer your spoon and the harder you gruel with more grease to your elbow the merrier fumes your new Irish stew.

JAMES JOYCE
Finnegans Wake

IRISH STEW

For centuries, the principal cooking utensils in Irish country cottages were the iron pot and black iron skillet, both of which have been used in various forms since the time of the Celts. The pot was filled with water, and whatever meat, grain, or vegetable was available was added for day-long cooking. Today, lamb is the meat of choice in Ireland's national dish, Irish Stew, and the recipe has spawned interesting variations that use lamb shanks instead of lamb cubes, turnips instead of carrots, and stout instead of stock. Most agree, however, that this recipe is a classic version. Serve it with Brown Soda Bread (page 41).

- 2 tbsp. canola oil
- 2 1/4 lb./1 kg boneless lamb, cut into 1/2 inch/1 cm pieces
- 2 large onions, sliced
- 2–3 large carrots, sliced
- 2–3 stalks celery, sliced
- 1 small turnip, cut into 1 inch/2.5 cm pieces (optional)
- 2–3 large baking potatoes, peeled and thickly sliced
- salt and freshly ground pepper to taste
- 1 tbsp. chopped fresh thyme
- chopped fresh flat-leaf parsley for garnish
- 1 1/2 cups/350 ml homemade chicken stock or canned low-sodium chicken broth

1. Preheat the oven to 300°F/150°C.
2. In a Dutch oven or large saucepan over medium heat, heat the oil. Working in batches, cook the lamb for about 5 minutes or until all the meat is browned.
3. In a flameproof casserole, alternate layers of meat, onions, carrots, celery, turnip (if using), and potatoes, ending with potatoes. Sprinkle each layer with salt, pepper, thyme, and some of the parsley.
4. Add the stock or broth and cover tightly with a lid. Cook for 2–2 1/2 hours or until the meat and vegetables are tender and the stock has thickened. Check the dish occasionally and add more stock or broth if necessary.
5. To serve, ladle stew into shallow bowls and sprinkle with the remaining parsley.

BEEF AND GUINNESS STEW

THIS Guinness-enriched beef stew is another Irish "standard," and it's a great make-ahead meal for a busy family. Raisins and caraway seeds offer a unique flavor to the stew, and cooks can feel free to add more or less of the vegetables to suit personal taste. Serve it with Brown Soda Bread (page 41) and Boiled New Potatoes (page 109).

- 2 tbsp. canola oil
- 2 tbsp. salted Irish butter
- 4 tbsp. all-purpose flour
- 2 lb./900 g boneless chuck beef, cut into 1 inch/2.5 cm cubes
- 4 medium onions, chopped
- 1 tbsp. tomato paste
- 4 cups/1 L homemade beef stock or canned low-salt beef broth
- 1 (11.2 oz.) bottle Guinness draught
- 1 tsp. caraway seeds
- 1 tbsp. raisins
- salt and freshly ground pepper to taste
- 5–6 large carrots, thickly sliced
- 4–5 large parsnips, thickly sliced
- 1 medium turnip, cut into 1 inch/2.5 cm pieces
- 2 tbsp. minced fresh flat-leaf parsley for garnish

1. In a Dutch oven or large saucepan over medium heat, heat the oil and butter.
2. Dredge the beef in flour and, working in batches, cook for about 5 minutes or until all the meat is browned. With a slotted spoon, remove the meat and reserve.
3. Add the onions to the pan and cook for 3–5 minutes, stirring occasionally, or until soft but not browned. Stir in the tomato paste and then stir in the broth and beer, scraping up the browned bits from the bottom of the pan. Return meat to pan and stir in the caraway seeds and raisins. Season with salt and pepper and bring to a boil.
4. Cover, reduce heat, and simmer for 1 hour, stirring occasionally. Uncover and bring to a boil. Cook for 20 minutes or until it thickens.
5. Add carrots, parsnips, and turnips. Cover, reduce heat to low, and simmer for 30 minutes, stirring occasionally.
6. Uncover and cook for 10–15 minutes longer or until the vegetables are tender and the stew thickens. (Prepare and chill the stew up to 1 day in advance; reheat on stovetop or in Crockpot).
7. To serve, ladle stew into shallow bowls, sprinkle with parsley, and serve with potatoes.

SHEPHERD'S PIE WITH CHEDDAR CRUST

Iɴ a land where sheep were traditionally a primary food supply, it's not surprising that lamb is the foundation for many farmhouse dishes. Shepherd's Pie, a long-time favorite, was originally created as an economical way to use leftover lamb and was always a favorite with farmers. This meat and vegetable pie is topped with a crust of mashed potatoes—here flavored with cheddar cheese—rather than pastry.

- 3 tbsp. canola oil
- 2 lb./900 g ground lamb
- 1 tbsp. salted Irish butter
- 1 large onion, chopped
- 1 clove garlic, crushed
- 3 carrots, diced
- 2 small tomatoes, peeled, seeded, and chopped
- 2 tbsp. tomato paste
- 1 1/2 tbsp. all-purpose flour
- 1 cup/250 ml homemade beef stock or canned low-sodium beef broth
- 1 tbsp. chopped fresh thyme
- 1 tbsp. chopped fresh flat-leaf parsley
- salt and freshly ground pepper
- 3 cups/750 g mashed potatoes
- 2 tbsp. salted Irish butter
- 1 cup/115 g grated Kerrygold Aged Cheddar cheese

1. In a large skillet over medium heat, heat the oil. Working in batches, cook the lamb for 5–7 minutes per batch or until all the meat is browned. With a slotted spoon, transfer the meat to a large bowl and reserve. Discard the fat.
2. Melt the butter in the same skillet. Add the onion, garlic, and carrots and cook for 3–5 minutes or until soft but not browned. Stir in the tomatoes, tomato paste, and flour, and then stir in the broth, thyme, and parsley, scraping up the browned bits from the bottom of the pan. Stir in the lamb.
3. Reduce the heat and simmer uncovered, stirring occasionally, for 10–15 minutes or until the mixture thickens. Season with salt and pepper.
4. Preheat the oven to 350°F/180°C. Spray an 8 inch/20 cm baking dish with cooking oil spray. Spoon the mixture into the prepared pan.
5. In a medium bowl, stir together the mashed potatoes and half the cheese. Decoratively spread or pipe the mashed potatoes over the meat mixture and sprinkle the remaining cheese over the top.
6. Bake for 25–30 minutes or until the top is browned and the mixture is bubbling. Serve immediately.

KERRY LAMB PIE

THE traditional Kerry Lamb Pie was originally made with stewed mutton and had both a top and bottom crust, somewhat like a turnover, dumpling, or Cornish pasty. This updated version is similar to a chicken potpie and uses puff pastry as a topping.

- 4 tbsp. salted Irish butter
- 8–10 large white mushrooms, halved
- 1 1/2 lb./750 g lamb, cut into 1 inch/2.5 cm pieces
- 2 tbsp. canola oil
- salt and freshly ground pepper to taste
- 1 clove garlic, chopped
- 1 large onion, chopped
- 2 stalks celery, chopped
- 3 carrots, chopped
- 2 parsnips, chopped
- 2 tbsp. tomato purée
- 3 cups/750 ml homemade chicken stock or canned low-sodium chicken broth
- 3/4 cup/175 ml dry white wine
- 1 tsp. gravy browning liquid, such as Kitchen Bouquet or Gravy Master brand
- *bouquet garni* (see Note)
- 1 sheet frozen puff pastry, defrosted according to package directions
- 1 egg beaten with 1 tbsp. water

NOTE: Bouquet garni is a French herbal mixture generally made with 1 bay leaf, 3 sprigs of thyme, and 4 sprigs of parsley. Gather the herbs together and tie them onto a 4 inch/10 cm piece of celery or place them into a sachet of cheesecloth.

1. In a small skillet over medium heat, melt 2 tbsp. of the butter. Add the mushrooms and cook for 3–5 minutes or until soft but not browned. Transfer the mushrooms to a bowl and reserve.
2. In a large saucepan or Dutch oven over medium heat, heat the oil and remaining 2 tbsp. butter. Add the lamb and cook for 4–5 minutes or until the lamb is browned on all sides. Season with salt and pepper.
3. Add the garlic, onions, celery, carrots, and parsnips, and cook, stirring constantly, for 5–7 minutes or until the vegetables are soft but not browned.
4. Stir in the tomato purée and cook for about 2 minutes or until the vegetables are coated. Add the stock or broth, wine, browning liquid, and *bouquet garni*.
5. Bring to a boil and then reduce the heat, cover, and simmer for 40 minutes. Uncover and then cook for 15–20 minutes more or until the lamb is tender and the mixture is thick. Remove the *bouquet garni* and stir in the reserved mushrooms.
6. Preheat the oven to 400°F/200°C. Spoon the lamb mixture into four 2 cup/500 ml ovenproof bowls.
7. On a floured surface, gently roll out the dough to smooth the folds. Using a saucer as a guide, cut out 4 rounds of pastry about 1 inch/2/5 cm larger than the bowl. Brush the egg wash on the bottom side, cover the pie, and then brush the egg wash on top.
8. Bake for 18–20 minutes or until the top is browned and the mixture is bubbling. Serve immediately.

CHICKEN AND HAM PIE

CLEVER cooks have always used leftover chicken and vegetables to make a savory pie, but this recipe takes it one step further and adds leftover ham as well. You can make the pie in a family-sized casserole dish or in smaller ovenproof dishes as in the recipe for Kerry Lamb Pie (page 87).

- 1 cup cooked chicken, cut into 1/2 inch/1 cm pieces
- 1 cup cooked ham, cut into 1/2 inch/1 cm pieces
- 8–10 large white mushrooms, diced
- 1 cup cooked peas
- 1 cup cooked carrot slices
- 4 tbsp. unsalted Irish butter
- 4 tbsp. all-purpose flour
- 2 cups/500 ml homemade chicken stock or canned low-salt chicken broth
- 1/2 cup/125 ml half-and-half
- salt and freshly ground pepper to taste
- 2 tbsp. minced fresh flat-leaf parsley
- 1 sheet frozen puff pastry, defrosted according to package directions
- 1 large egg beaten with 1 tbsp. water

1. Preheat the oven to 400°F/200°C. Generously grease a 2 quart/2 L ovenproof casserole dish and put the chicken and ham into the dish. Scatter the mushrooms, peas, and carrots over the meat.
2. In a medium saucepan over medium heat, melt the butter. Whisk in the flour, and then slowly whisk in the stock or broth. Bring to a boil and cook, whisking constantly, for 3–5 minutes or until thick and smooth. Season with salt and pepper and stir in the parsley. Pour the sauce over the meat and vegetables and let cool for about 15 minutes.
3. On a floured surface, gently roll out the dough to smooth the folds. Cut a piece to fit the top of the dish and make slits in it to let out the steam as the pie bakes.
4. Brush some of the egg wash on the bottom side, cover the pie, and then brush the remaining egg wash on top. Press the dough down along the edge of the dish to seal.
5. Bake for 10 minutes and then reduce the heat to 350°F/180°C and bake for 15 minutes longer or until the top is browned and the mixture is bubbling. Serve immediately.

LOUGH ESKE COTTAGE PIE

Lough Eske Castle in Donegal Town dates to the 1400s and is long associated with the O'Donnell's, founding fathers of Ireland's northwestern most county. Set on 43 acres of forest and bordering the shores of Lough Eske, the Tudor-baronial castle, the only five-star hotel in Co. Donegal, was refurbished in 2007 and is now a member of the Solis Hotel group. Head Chef Philipp Ferber is noted for serving easy-going meals, like this classic Cottage Pie, in both the Gallery Bar and Oak Bar.

- 3 tbsp. olive oil
- 2 lb./900 g ground beef
- 5 tbsp. Worcestershire sauce
- 1/2 cup/125 ml dry red wine
- 1 tbsp. salted Irish butter
- 1 large onion, chopped
- 1 clove garlic, crushed
- 3 carrots, grated
- 2 tbsp. tomato paste
- 1 1/2 tbsp. all-purpose flour
- 1 cup/250 ml homemade chicken stock or canned low-salt chicken broth
- 2 tbsp. chopped fresh thyme
- salt and freshly ground pepper to taste
- 3 cups/750 g mashed potatoes
- 2 large egg yolks
- 2 tbsp. salted Irish butter
- 1/2 tsp. English mustard
- 1/4 cup/30 g grated Dubliner cheese

1. In a large skillet over medium heat, heat the oil. Working in batches, cook the beef for 5–7 minutes or until all the meat is browned. Transfer the beef to a colander to drain.
2. Add the Worcestershire sauce and wine to the skillet and cook, scraping up the browned bits from the bottom of the pan, for about 10 minutes or until reduced by half. Reserve.
3. In a large skillet over medium heat, melt the butter. Add the onion, garlic, and carrots and cook for 3–5 minutes or until soft but not browned. Stir in the tomato paste and flour and then stir in the broth and thyme. Stir in the beef and reserved cooking liquid.
4. Reduce the heat and simmer uncovered, stirring occasionally, for 10–15 minutes or until the mixture thickens. Season with salt and pepper.
5. Preheat the oven to 350°F/180°C. Spray an 8 inch/20 cm baking dish with cooking oil spray. Spoon the mixture into the prepared pan.
6. In a medium bowl, stir together the mashed potatoes, butter, egg yolks, and mustard. Decoratively spread or pipe the mashed potatoes over the meat mixture and sprinkle the cheese over the top.
7. Bake for 20–25 minutes or until the top is browned and the mixture is bubbling. Serve immediately.

Photo courtesy of Fermanagh Black Bacon Cookbook

FERMANAGH BLACK BACON AND POTATO PIE

PAT O'Doherty is possibly the most well known butcher in all of Co. Fermanagh, not only for the quality of his meats in general but for his special breed of free range pigs reared on Inishcorkish Island in Upper Lough Erne. O'Doherty's pigs forage naturally on grass, wild herbs, roots, and shrubs, a diet and habitat that results in a superior bacon called Fermanagh Black Bacon. After a personal visit to his Enniskillen shop earlier this year, I convinced him to share some of his recipes, including this hearty pie made with bacon and potatoes. The recipe is adapted from his *Fermanagh Black Bacon Cookbook*.

- 10 tbsp. salted Irish butter
- 8 slices Fermanagh Black Bacon, or similar brand, chopped
- 4 large baking potatoes, peeled and thinly sliced
- 3 shallots, finely chopped
- freshly ground pepper to taste
- 2 tbsp. fresh tarragon
- 2 tbsp. chopped fresh chives
- 2 sheets frozen puff pastry, defrosted according to package directions
- 2 large egg yolks, beaten
- 1 cup/250 ml heavy (whipping) cream

1. Preheat the oven to 350°F/ 200°C. Line a baking sheet with parchment paper.
2. In a large skillet over medium heat, melt 5 tbsp. of the butter. Add the bacon and cook for 8–10 minutes or until browned.
3. Add the potatoes to the skillet and cook, stirring constantly, for 8–10 minutes or until nearly tender. Transfer the bacon and potatoes to a bowl and reserve.
4. Melt the remaining 5 tbsp. of the butter in the same skillet. Add the shallots and cook for 2–3 minutes or until soft but not browned. Season with pepper and then stir in the tarragon and chives. Stir into the potato and bacon mixture.
5. On a lightly floured surface, roll out one piece of pastry to a 12 inch/30 cm circle. Brush the edges with some of the egg yolk. Spread the potato mixture over the pastry, leaving a 2 inch/5 cm border.
6. Roll out the remaining piece of the pastry to a slightly larger circle. Put it over the filling and crimp the edges inward to seal it.
7. With a biscuit cutter, cut out a circle from the middle of the pie but do not remove it. Brush the top with the rest of the egg yolk. Bake for 40–45 minutes or until the top is golden. If the top browns too quickly, cover with aluminum foil.
8. In a small saucepan over medium heat, heat the cream. Remove the pie from the oven and remove the small circle from the middle. Pour in the hot cream and return to the oven for 10 minutes or until the mixture is bubbling. Slice and serve immediately.

Photo courtesy of Bord Bia

BACON-LEEK TART

LEEKS, a popular member of the onion family, are one of the oldest Irish vegetables. They combine well with everything from fish and fowl to meat and potatoes and are particularly delicious in this bacon and potato tart with a creamy egg and cheese filling. If you prefer a shortcut, use refrigerated pie dough instead of the pastry.

FILLING

- 8 slices Irish breakfast bacon, chopped
- 2 tbsp. salted Irish butter
- 4 leeks (white part only), washed and sliced
- 6 large eggs
- 1 (8 oz./225 g) package cream cheese, at room temperature
- 1 tbsp. Lakeshore French Mustard or similar brand
- 1/4 tsp. cayenne pepper
- salt and freshly ground pepper to taste

TART PASTRY

- 1 1/4 cups/300 g all-purpose flour
- pinch of salt
- 8 tbsp. unsalted Irish butter, cut into small pieces
- 1 large egg yolk
- 2 tbsp. cold water

1. Into a food processor fitted with a metal blade, sift the flour and salt. Add the butter and pulse 8–10 times or until the mixture resembles fine breadcrumbs. With the machine running, add the egg yolk and just enough water to combine the dough.
2. Turn the dough out onto a lightly floured surface and press the dough into a ball. Wrap in plastic and refrigerate for 1 hour and up to 3 days. (The dough can be frozen at this point for up to 2 months.)
3. Preheat the oven to 400°F/200°C. On a lightly floured surface, roll out the dough to a 12 inch/30 cm circle. Press the dough into a tart pan with removable bottom, leaving a 1/2 inch/1 cm overhang around the rim.
4. Fold in the excess dough to form thick edges. Prick the bottom with a fork and refrigerate for about 15 minutes. Cut a piece of foil or parchment to fit the pan, and top with pie weights or dried beans. Bake for 18–20 minutes or until the edges are lightly browned.
5. Remove weights and parchment and bake for 10–15 minutes more, or until the bottom is browned. Remove from the oven and let cool in the pan on a wire rack.
6. Reduce heat to 350°F/180°C.
7. To make the filling, in a large skillet over medium heat, cook the bacon, turning frequently, for 7–9 minutes or until lightly browned. Set aside.
8. Melt the butter in the same skillet, add the leeks, and cook for 3–4 minutes or until soft but not browned. Remove from the heat.
9. In a large bowl, whisk together the eggs, cream cheese, mustard, cayenne pepper, salt, and pepper. Stir in the leeks and bacon. Pour the filling into the pastry shell and bake for 35–40 minutes or until the filling is firm. Remove from the oven and let cool for about 5 minutes before cutting into slices.

Photo courtesy of Cakebread Cellars and Food & Wine Magazine

CARAMELIZED ONION AND BLUE CHEESE TART

THREE of Dublin's most popular restaurants—Ely Chq Brasserie (Custom House Quay), Ely Hq Gastro Pub (Hanover Quay), and Ely Winebar (22 Ely Place)—use the best of seasonal Irish produce, organic where possible, from the Ely family farm in the Burren, Co. Clare. Head chef Ryan Stringer favors a classic brasserie menu in all of the restaurants, like this very smart tart that features Cashel Blue, Ireland's original blue cheese from Co. Tipperary. The Ely restaurants and Cashel Blue Farmhouse Cheese are members of Good Food Ireland.

FILLING

- 4 tbsp. olive oil
- 2 large red onions, thinly sliced
- 1 tbsp. fresh thyme leaves
- 1 tbsp. brown sugar
- 2 tbsp. balsamic vinegar
- 4 oz./115 g Cashel Blue cheese, crumbled
- 2 cups/500 ml heavy (whipping) cream
- 6 large egg yolks
- pinch of nutmeg
- salt and freshly ground pepper to taste
- thyme sprigs for garnish

TART PASTRY

- 1 1/4 cups/300 g all-purpose flour
- pinch of salt
- 8 tbsp. unsalted Irish butter, cut into small pieces
- 1 large egg yolk
- 2 tbsp. cold water

1. Into a food processor fitted with a metal blade, sift the flour and salt. Add the butter and pulse 8–10 times or until the mixture resembles fine breadcrumbs. With the machine running, add the egg yolk and just enough water to combine the dough.
2. Turn the dough out onto a lightly floured surface and press the dough into a ball. Wrap in plastic and refrigerate for 1 hour and up to 3 days. (The dough can be frozen at this point for up to 2 months.)
3. Preheat the oven to 400°F/200°C. On a lightly floured surface, roll out the dough to a 12 inch/30 cm circle. Press the dough into a tart pan with removable bottom, leaving a 1/2 inch/1 cm overhang around the rim.
4. Fold in the excess dough to form thick edges. Prick the bottom with a fork and refrigerate for about 15 minutes. Cut a piece of foil or parchment to fit the pan, and top with pie weights or dried beans. Bake for 18–20 minutes or until the edges are lightly browned.
5. Remove weights and parchment and bake for 10–15 minutes more, or until the bottom is browned. Remove from the oven and let cool in the pan on a wire rack.
6. Reduce heat to 350°F/180°C.
7. To make the filling, in a large skillet over medium heat, heat the olive oil. Add the onions and thyme and cook for 3–5 minutes or until the onions are soft but not browned. Add the sugar and cook for 5 minutes. Add the vinegar, stir, and remove from the heat. Let cool.
8. Strain off excess liquid and spread the onion mixture evenly over the pastry. Sprinkle the cheese over the onions.
9. In a medium bowl, whisk together the cream, egg yolks, nutmeg, salt, and pepper. Pour over the cheese and onions and bake for 35–40 minutes or until the top is golden and the filling is set.
10. To serve, cut into slices and garnish with thyme sprigs.

The team @ Fishy Fishy

FISHY FISHY PIE

MARTIN Shanahan is mad about fish and has turned his passion into a national phenomenon. In 1991, the Tipperary-trained chef opened Fishy Fishy as a fish shop and deli in Kinsale, Co. Cork. It became one of Ireland's most successful and acclaimed restaurants, and Shanahan expanded his business by opening Fishy Fishy Café eight years later. Now with a cookbook and popular RTE television series, "Martin's Mad About Fish," he's put his mantra of "no skin, no bones, no fear" into the psyche of a huge audience who have discovered the pleasures of cooking great fish and shellfish. His fisherman's pie, adapted here from *Martin's Fishy Fishy Cookbook*, is a great example of how to use four or five different species in one dish. Fishy Fishy Café is a member of Good Food Ireland.

- 4 cups/1 L fish stock
- 1 cup/250 ml light cream
- 2 tbsp. all-purpose flour
- 4 tbsp. salted Irish butter
- 1 tbsp. dried mustard
- salt and freshly ground pepper to taste
- 1 tbsp. canola oil
- 2 lb./900 g fresh fish (haddock, monkfish, cod), skinned, boned, and cut into cubes
- 1/4 lb./115 g shrimp, peeled
- 1 small leek (white part only), sliced
- 1 large carrot, grated
- 3 tbsp. minced fresh flat-leaf parsley, plus more for garnish
- 1 lb./450 g mashed potatoes
- 2 tbsp. salted Irish butter
- grated Parmesan cheese for topping

1. Preheat the oven to 325°F/170°C. Generously grease an ovenproof casserole dish.
2. In a medium saucepan over medium heat, gently bring the stock and cream to a boil.
3. In a small bowl, combine the flour and 2 tbsp. of the butter to make a roux. Beat the roux, piece by piece, into the liquid and cook for 3–5 minutes or until the sauce thickens. Stir in the mustard and season with salt and pepper.
4. In a large skillet over medium heat, heat the oil. Sauté the fish and shrimp for about 3 minutes or until nearly cooked through. Stir in the leek, carrot, and parsley and then stir in the sauce. Transfer the mixture to the prepared dish and spread the mashed potatoes over the top. Dot with the remaining 2 tbsp. butter and sprinkle with the grated cheese. Bake for 15–20 minutes or until the top is browned and the mixture is bubbling.
5. To serve, spoon into shallow bowls and garnish with parsley.

SMOKED SALMON TART

Always popular, smoked salmon can be as simple or as sumptuous as the occasion demands. In Ireland, where oak-smoked salmon is regarded as a national treasure, it appears on menus everywhere, including in tarts like this that are perfect for a light lunch or casual supper.

- 1 sheet frozen puff pastry, defrosted according to package directions
- 2 tbsp. salted Irish butter
- 2 shallots, finely chopped
- 2 large eggs, beaten
- 1/2 cup/125 ml half-and-half
- freshly ground black pepper to taste
- 6 slices Irish oak-smoked salmon, finely chopped
- 1 tbsp. chopped fresh dill
- fresh chive sprigs for garnish

1. Roll dough out to fit a 9 inch/22 cm round or 8x11 inch/20x27.5 cm rectangular tart pan with removable bottom, leaving a 1 inch/2.5 cm overhang. Fold in the excess dough to make thick sides. Prick the bottom with a fork and chill for 30 minutes.
2. Preheat the oven to 375°F/190°C. Line the pastry with a piece of aluminum foil or parchment paper. Fill with pie weights or beans and bake for 18–20 minutes or until the crust is set. Remove foil and weights and bake for 10–12 minutes longer or until the crust edges are golden (pierce with a fork if crust bubbles).
3. In a large skillet over medium heat, melt the butter. Cook the shallots for 3–5 minutes or until soft but not browned. Set aside.
4. In a small bowl, whisk together the eggs and half-and-half. Season with pepper.
5. Sprinkle the salmon evenly over the bottom of the pastry. Sprinkle the shallots and dill over the salmon, and then pour in the eggs mixture. Bake for 30–40 minutes or until the custard is set.
6. To serve, remove from the oven and let cool for about 5 minutes before cutting into slices. Garnish with chive sprigs.

ARDSALLAGH GOAT'S CHEESE, WILD MUSHROOM, AND ASPARAGUS TART

THERE are a number of goat cheesemakers in Ireland today, but after a visit to Jane and Gerard Murphy's delightful farm in Carrigtwohill, Co. Cork, I fell in love with their range of Ardsallagh products made from the milk of their mixed herd of Saanan, Anglo-Nubian, and Alpine goats. The cheeses include soft goat's cheese, fresh and creamy due to hand ladling; hard cheese that becomes saltier and more nutty as the cheese ages; and smoked cheese, sweet and mild when young, nuttier when aged. This tart combines their soft cheese with the strong flavors of roasted asparagus and sautéed wild mushrooms. Ardsallagh Goat Farm is a member of Good Food Ireland.

- 1 lb./450 g asparagus, trimmed and peeled
- 4 tbsp. olive oil
- sea salt to taste
- 8 oz./225 g Ardsallagh goat's cheese
- 1 large egg yolk
- 4 tbsp. crème frâiche
- 1 tbsp. salted Irish butter
- 1 1/2 lb./750 g chopped mushrooms
- 2 shallots, minced
- 2 tsp. fresh thyme
- salt and freshly ground pepper to taste
- 1 sheet frozen puff pastry, defrosted according to package directions
- 1 large egg yolk mixed with 1 tbsp. water

1. Preheat the oven to 400°F/200°C.
2. Arrange the asparagus in a single layer on a baking sheet. Drizzle with 1 tbsp. of the olive oil, sprinkle with the salt, and toss to coat. Bake for 18–20 minutes or until tender. Remove from the oven and set aside.
3. In a food processor, combine half of the goat's cheese, egg yolk, and 1 tbsp. of the olive oil. Process for 30 seconds or until smooth. Transfer to a bowl and fold in the crème frâiche.
4. In a large skillet over medium heat, heat the remaining 2 tbsp. of the olive oil and the butter. Add the mushrooms and shallots and cook for 5–7 minutes or until soft but not browned. Add the thyme, and season with salt and pepper.
5. On a lightly floured surface, roll out the pastry to a 12x8 inch/30x20 cm rectangle. With a sharp knife, score a line 1/4 inch/5 mm around the sides of the dough, cutting halfway through. Brush the border with the egg wash. Spread the goat cheese mixture over the dough up to the border.
6. Arrange the roasted asparagus lengthwise across the tart in a single layer up to the border. Top with the mushrooms and then crumble the remaining goat cheese over the top. Bake for about 25 minutes or until the crust is golden.
7. To serve, cut into squares and serve immediately.

O 'Donnab

BED & BREAKFAST

BAR

BED & BREAKFA

B&B RECEPTION

B&B
Lóistín Oíche

FOOD
ALL DAY

GUINNESS

le gach Béile

Bar Entrance

DINNER TIME

The food of Ireland is like the Irish people: unpretentious and homely. Simple and succulent dishes have been a tradition for centuries and are still an important part of Irish life. What Gernow, Second Justice of the Province of Munster, said in 1620 could still be quoted with truth today: "What feeds on earth, or flies in the air, Or swimmeth in the water, Lo, Ireland hath it of her own."

THEODORA FITZGIBBON
A Taste of Ireland

Photo courtesy of Bord Bia

LEG OF LAMB WITH HONEY-ORANGE GLAZE, PORT, AND MINT DRESSING

SHEEP farming is an age-old tradition in Ireland. Thanks to the country's mild weather, lambs (sheep that are 12 months old or younger) spend most of the year outside and primarily feed off grass with little cereal supplementation. Lamb is also one of Ireland's most popular meats, and the ways to prepare it seem endless. This flavorful leg of lamb, based on a recipe from Bord Bia (Irish Food Board), is often reserved for special occasions and served with elegant Dauphinoise Potatoes (page 117), a make-ahead casserole also known as "scalloped" or "au gratin" potatoes.

- 2 medium onions, chopped
- 1 whole garlic, peeled and cut in half
- 1 garlic clove, peeled and crushed
- 1 tbsp. salt
- 2 tbsp. orange zest
- 2 tbsp. Mileeven Irish Honey or similar brand
- 2 tbsp. olive oil
- 1 (5 lb./2 kg) leg of lamb
- 3 garlic cloves, peeled and cut into slivers
- rosemary sprigs
- 1/2 cup/125 ml dry white wine
- 1/2 cup/125 ml water

PORT AND MINT DRESSING

- reserved pan juices
- 4 tbsp. redcurrant jelly
- 1/2 cup/125 ml orange juice
- 1 tbsp. port
- 4–5 mint sprigs, plus additional for garnish
- 1 tbsp. salted Irish butter
- salt and freshly ground pepper to taste

1. Bring the reserved pan juices, jelly, juice, port, and mint to a boil. Cook for 3–5 minutes or until slightly thickened, and then whisk in the butter.
2. Cook for about 5 minutes more or until the sauce is smooth. Season with salt and pepper.

1. Preheat the oven to 400°F/200°C. Place the onions and garlic halves in the bottom of a large roasting pan.
2. In a small bowl, combine the crushed garlic, salt, orange zest, honey, and oil. Spread the mixture over the lamb and put the lamb in the roasting pan.
3. Make about 10 incisions in the lamb and place a sliver of garlic and a small sprig of rosemary in each. Roast for 30 minutes. Add the wine and water to the pan, reduce the temperature to 350°F/180°C, and roast for 1 hour longer.
4. Remove the lamb from the roasting pan and let rest for 15 minutes. Reserve the garlic to serve with the lamb and strain the juices into a small saucepan.
5. To serve, slice the lamb and serve with the dressing and potatoes.

RACK OF LAMB WITH GUINNESS AND MUSTARD

A rack of lamb is the ultimate special occasion cut. A "rack" usually consists of about 8 ribs, the bones of which are scraped clean for a lovely presentation. Ask your butcher to "French" (trim) the racks for you, and then marinate them in Guinness before roasting. The mustard adds flavor to the lamb and helps the breadcrumbs stick. This is a popular dish at The Guinness Storehouse in Dublin, where the chef promises, "Guinness is the only beer that really makes this work. The glaze on the lamb is as rich as you'd expect from red wine." Serve this with Champ (page 107) and Honey-Glazed Carrots (recipe follows). The Brewery Bar is a member of Good Food Ireland.

- 2 (1 1/2 lb./750 g) French-trimmed racks of lamb (8 ribs each)
- 2/3 cup/150 ml Guinness draught beer
- 2 tbsp. Lakeshore French Mustard or similar brand
- 5 tbsp. seasoned breadcrumbs

1. In a large bowl, combine the lamb and Guinness. Cover and refrigerate for 6–8 hours or overnight.
2. Preheat the oven to 400°F/200°C. Remove the lamb from the marinade and pat dry. Coat with the mustard and press the breadcrumbs over the lamb.
3. Place the lamb on a rack and bake for 20–25 minutes or until a meat thermometer inserted into the thickest part of the lamb registers 130°F/54°C. Remove from the oven and let rest for about 10 minutes.
4. To serve, cut the rack into chops and serve with the carrots and potatoes.

HONEY-GLAZED CARROTS

- 1 lb./450 g baby carrots
- 1 tbsp. salted Irish butter
- 1 tbsp. orange marmalade
- 1 tbsp. Mileeven Irish Honey or similar brand
- 1/4 tsp. chopped fresh rosemary
- 1/4 tsp. chopped fresh thyme
- salt and freshly ground pepper to taste

1. In a medium saucepan, cook the carrots in salted boiling water for about 10 minutes or until tender. Drain and return to saucepan.
2. In a small saucepan over medium heat, combine the butter, marmalade, and honey. Cook for 3–5 minutes or until melted and smooth. Stir in the rosemary and thyme and then stir into the carrots. Season with salt and pepper and heat through.

Serves 6–8

BRAISED LAMB SHANKS

Noel McMeel honed his cooking skills with American chefs like Alice Waters and the late Jean-Louis Palladin before returning to Northern Ireland, where he now serves as Executive Head Chef at Lough Erne Resort, Enniskillen, Co. Fermanagh. Always noted for his eclectic interpretations of traditional recipes, the chef braises these hearty shanks in red wine and tomatoes and serves them with Champ (recipe follows), a traditional dish of mashed potatoes and scallions or chives. Lough Erne Resort is a member of Good Food Ireland.

- 3 tbsp. olive oil
- 4 (12 oz./350 g) lamb shanks
- 1 large carrot, chopped
- 1 large onion, chopped
- 1 stalk celery, chopped
- 1/2 cup/125 ml dry red wine
- 1/2 cup/125 ml chopped tomatoes
- 4–5 sprigs thyme
- 1 bay leaf
- 1 small garlic, peeled and chopped
- 1 cup/250 ml water
- salt and freshly ground pepper to taste

1. In a large skillet over medium heat, heat the olive oil. Cook the lamb on all sides for 5–8 minutes or until browned. Transfer to a Dutch oven.
2. Add the carrot, onion, and celery to the skillet and cook for 5 minutes, stirring to scrape up the browned bits from the bottom of the pan. Add the wine.
3. Transfer the cooked vegetables and pan juices to the lamb in the Dutch oven. Add the tomatoes, thyme, bay leaf, garlic, water, salt, and pepper, then cover and simmer for about 2 hours or until the lamb is nearly tender.
4. Remove the lamb shanks from the Dutch oven and transfer to a platter. Cover and keep warm. Strain the sauce through a fine sieve into a clean saucepan, pressing the vegetables through with the back of a large spoon. Cook over low heat for about 5 minutes or until the sauce thickens.
5. To serve, place a lamb shank in the center of each of 4 serving plates, spoon the sauce over, and serve with the potatoes.

CHAMP

- 4 large baking potatoes, peeled and cut into 1 1/2 inch/3.5 cm pieces
- 1/2 cup/125 ml half-and-half
- 6 tbsp. salted Irish butter
- 1 cup/115 g minced scallions or chives
- salt and freshly ground pepper to taste

1. Cook the potatoes in salted boiling water for about 20 minutes or until tender. Drain and mash. In a medium saucepan over low heat, combine the half-and-half and 4 tbsp. of the butter. Heat until the butter melts.
2. Add the scallions or chives, reduce heat to simmer, and cook for 2–4 minutes or until softened.
3. Stir the milk mixture into the potatoes and season with salt and pepper. Top with the remaining 2 tbsp. butter.

Serves 8

LAMB CUTLETS WITH HONEY-APRICOT SAUCE

THIS easy-to-prepare recipe is a lovely way to showcase delicate lamb cutlets or loin chops. The sauce can be made ahead and reheated while the lamb is cooking, and Garlic-Herb Mash (recipe follows) nicely complements the sweet-tart taste of the lamb and sauce.

- 4 oz./115 g dried apricots, chopped
- 2 cups/500 ml homemade chicken stock or canned chicken broth
- 2 tbsp. minced fresh tarragon
- 2 1/2 tbsp. Mileeven Irish Honey or similar brand
- 2 tsp. fresh lemon juice
- salt and freshly ground pepper to taste
- 1 tsp. hot Thai curry paste
- 2 tbsp. olive oil
- 12 lamb cutlets or loin chops
- tarragon sprigs for garnish

1. Soak the apricots and tarragon in the stock or broth for 3–4 hours. Transfer to a food processor, add 1 tbsp. of the honey, lemon juice, salt, and pepper, and process until smooth.
2. In a small saucepan over medium heat, cook the apricot mixture for 2–3 minutes or until heated through.
3. Light a fire in a charcoal grill or preheat a gas grill to medium–high.
4. In a small bowl, combine the remaining honey, curry paste, and olive oil. Brush the mixture over both sides of the lamb and season with salt and pepper. Grill for 3 minutes on each side for rare, 5 minutes on each side for medium.
5. To serve, arrange 3 cutlets on each of 4 serving plates and spoon the sauce over. Garnish with tarragon sprigs and serve with the potatoes.

GARLIC-HERB MASH

- 4 large baking potatoes, peeled and cut into 1 1/2 inch/3.5 cm pieces
- 1/2 cup/125 ml half-and-half
- 6 tbsp. Kerrygold Garlic and Herb butter
- salt and freshly ground pepper to taste

1. Cook the potatoes in salted boiling water for about 20 minutes or until tender. Drain and mash. In a medium saucepan over low heat, combine the milk and butter. Heat until the butter melts and then stir into the potatoes. Season with salt and pepper. Reheat just before serving.

Serves 8

BACON AND CABBAGE WITH WHOLEGRAIN MUSTARD SAUCE

Bacon and Cabbage is one of Ireland's most traditional dishes. Boiled Potatoes (recipe follows) and carrots, which can be cooked with the cabbage or in separate saucepans, are the usual accompaniments, and sauces, like this made with Lakeshore (the number 1 producer of wholegrain mustard in Ireland), are nearly obligatory.

- 4 lb./1.8 kg boiling bacon, such as Tommy Moloney's brand
- 2 medium heads green cabbage, quartered
- boiled carrots for serving

1. Put the bacon in a large saucepan and cover with cold water. Bring the water slowly to a boil, cover, and then reduce the heat and simmer, skimming the water occasionally to remove foam, for 1 1/2 hours or until tender.
2. Add the cabbage and cook for 12–15 minutes or until the cabbage is tender (do not overcook).
3. Remove the bacon from the pot and cover with foil to keep warm. (Reserve 1 1/4 cups/300 ml of the cooking liquid). Drain the cabbage over a bowl and return to pot to keep warm.
4. To serve, slice the meat and serve with the cabbage, carrots, potatoes, and sauce.

WHOLEGRAIN MUSTARD SAUCE

- 2 tbsp. salted Irish butter
- 1 small shallot, chopped
- 2 tsp. Lakeshore Wholegrain Mustard or similar brand
- 2/3 cup/150 ml dry white wine
- 1 1/4 cups/300 ml reserved cooking liquid
- 1 1/4 cups/300 ml half-and-half
- freshly ground pepper to taste

1. In a medium saucepan over medium heat, melt the butter. Add the shallot and cook for 3–5 minutes or until soft but not browned. Stir in the mustard and wine and cook for 2 minutes.
2. Add the reserved cooking liquid and cook for about 5 minutes or until reduced by half. Add the half-and-half and cook for 5 minutes longer or until the sauce is thickened. Season with pepper.

Makes about 2 cups

BOILED NEW POTATOES

- 3 lb./1.4 kg small boiling potatoes
- 2 tbsp. unsalted Irish butter
- minced fresh flat-leaf parsley for topping
- salt and freshly ground pepper to taste

1. Cook the potatoes in salted boiling water for about 15 minutes or until tender. Drain and return to the pan to dry out a little. Top with the butter, parsley, salt, and pepper.

Serves 6–8

MAGNERS GLAZED HAM

NOTHING beats a cider-glazed ham as the centerpiece of a buffet meal or holiday gathering. This recipe uses Magners, the U.S. brand of Bulmers, cider produced in Clonmel, Co. Tipperary, since 1935. The cider uses over 17 varieties of apples, is fermented using a unique yeast from the oak vats of the original Dowd's Lane Cider Mill, and is left to mature for up to 2 years. For drinking, most people prefer it served over ice; for cooking, many consider it to be as versatile as wine. Serve it with Potato, Parsnip, and Apple Purée (recipe follows).

- one butt half (6 lb./2.2 kg), bone-in, fully cooked ham
- 12–15 whole cloves
- 2 cups/500 ml Magners Irish Cider
- 4 tbsp. pineapple juice
- 2 tbsp. (packed) dark brown sugar
- 1 tbsp. Lakeshore French Mustard or similar brand

1. Preheat the oven to 325°F/170°C. Score the ham in a diamond pattern and stud with the cloves.
2. In a small bowl, combine the cider and pineapple juice. Place the ham, cut-side down, on a rack in a large roasting pan. Pour the cider mixture over the top. Loosely cover the ham with aluminum foil and bake for 1 1/2 hours.
3. In a small bowl, combine the brown sugar and mustard. Mix 3–4 tbsp. of the cooking liquid with the mustard mixture and spoon it over the ham.
4. Continue to cook, uncovered, basting frequently for 30–40 minutes or until an instant-read thermometer registers 160°F/70°C when inserted into the thickest part of the ham. Remove the ham to a platter or cutting board. Cover with foil and let stand for 10–15 minutes or longer.
5. To serve, cut the ham into slices and serve with the potato purée.

POTATO, PARSNIP, AND APPLE PURÉE

- 6–8 parsnips, thickly sliced
- 4 large baking potatoes, peeled and cut into 1 1/2 inch/3.5 cm pieces
- 1/2 cup/125 ml water
- 3 large cooking apples, peeled, cored, and sliced
- 1 cup/250 ml warm milk
- 12 tbsp. unsalted Irish butter, cut into pieces
- salt and freshly ground pepper to taste

1. Cook the parsnips and potatoes in a large saucepan of salted boiling water for 20–25 minutes or until tender. Drain and mash. Return to the saucepan.
2. In a medium saucepan over medium-low heat, cook the apples, covered, for 15–20 minutes or until tender. Drain and mash.
3. Stir the apples into the potato mixture and then stir in the milk and butter. With a hand mixer or immersion blender, blend until smooth. Season with salt and pepper. Reheat just before serving.

Serves 8

PORK SHOULDER SLOW-ROASTED IN MAGNERS WITH SAVOY CABBAGE

DOONBEG Lodge is situated in a coastal haven on a sheltered corner of the Atlantic Ocean in the village of Doonbeg, Co. Clare. One of the most breathtaking sites in all of Ireland, the 400-acre property (which includes a Greg Norman-designed golf course) sits on a mile-long stretch of beach on Doughmore Bay. After a challenging day of golf, guests delight in heading off to a deluxe meal prepared by Chef Wade Murphy before snuggling up in the luxurious Lodge. One of his signature dishes is this pork slow-roasted in Magners Irish Cider and served with a contemporary version of bacon and cabbage. Chef Murphy offers some cooking advice: "Cooking the pork slowly allows the fat to tender for better basting, and turning up the heat at the end of the cooking gives a crisp skin." He suggests a simple accompaniment of Boiled New Potatoes (page 109).

- 3 lb./1.4 kg boned pork shoulder
- 2 tbsp. canola oil
- sea salt for rubbing
- 1 medium onion, thickly sliced
- 1 large carrot, roughly chopped
- 1 stalk celery, roughly chopped
- 2 cups/500 ml homemade beef stock or canned low-salt beef broth
- 1 3/4 cups/425 ml Magners Irish Cider
- *bouquet garni* (page 87)
- 1 bay leaf
- 2 whole cloves
- salt and freshly ground pepper to taste

1. Preheat the oven to 450°F/230°C.
2. With a sharp knife, score the skin of the pork at 1/4 inch/5 mm intervals. Pour some boiling water over the top to aid with crisping the skin. Pat dry, rub the skin with oil, and sprinkle with salt.
3. Place the onion, carrot, and celery in a roasting pan and put the pork, skin side up, on top. Pour the stock and cider around the meat, and add the *bouquet garni*, bay leaf, and cloves. Season with salt and pepper. Roast the pork for about 20 minutes or until the skin starts to brown and crisp.
4. Reduce the temperature to 275°F/140°C and cook for 2–2 1/2 hours longer (if skin is browning too much, cover with aluminum foil for the last 45 minutes). Remove the meat from the oven and transfer to a plate.
5. Strain the vegetables and stock through a fine sieve into a small saucepan. Bring to a boil, and then reduce heat and simmer, skimming constantly, for 8–10 minutes or until the sauce thickens.
6. To serve, divide the cabbage onto 4 serving plates. Cut the meat into thick slices and place on top of the cabbage. Pour the sauce over the meat and serve with the potatoes.

CONTINUED ON NEXT PAGE

SAVOY CABBAGE

- 2 tbsp. unsalted Irish butter
- 2 shallots, peeled and finely chopped
- 3 slices Irish bacon, chopped
- 1 head Savoy cabbage, cored and thinly sliced
- 3/4 cup/175 ml dry white wine
- 2 tbsp. chopped fresh flat-leaf parsley
- salt and freshly ground pepper to taste
- 1 cooking apple, peeled and cored

1. In a large saucepan over medium heat, melt the butter. Stir in the shallots and bacon and cook for 3–5 minutes or until the shallots are soft and the bacon is lightly browned.
2. Stir in the cabbage and cook for about 2 minutes or until it begins to wilt. Stir in the wine, cover, and cook, stirring occasionally, for 5–6 minutes or until the cabbage is nearly tender. Add the parsley and grate the apple into the cabbage. Reheat just before serving.

Serves 4

BEEF TENDERLOIN WITH HORSERADISH-MUSTARD CRUST

I'T's safe to say that regardless of where you eat in Ireland—from five-star restaurants and hotels to country houses and pubs—you will find a great piece of Irish beef on the menu. The "best of the best" is center cut filet of beef, also known as beef tenderloin. Most agree the rather expensive cut of beef is well worth the price, though, not only because it's so easy to prepare but also because of its remarkable flavor. Serve this with Dauphinoise Potatoes (recipe follows).

- 2 tbsp. prepared horseradish
- 2 tbsp. Lakeshore Wholegrain Mustard or similar brand
- 2 tbsp. kosher salt
- freshly ground pepper to taste
- 1 tbsp. finely chopped garlic
- 1 tbsp. finely chopped shallot
- 1 tsp. chopped fresh thyme
- 2 tbsp. olive oil
- 1 (3 lb./1.4 kg) beef tenderloin, trimmed and patted dry

1. Preheat the oven to 400°F/200°C.
2. Combine the horseradish, mustard, salt, pepper, garlic, shallot, thyme, and olive oil in a food processor or blender and process until smooth. Rub the mixture over all sides of the beef and put it on a rack in a roasting pan.
3. Roast for about 40 minutes or until a meat thermometer inserted into the center of the beef registers 120°F/48°C (for rare) or 130°F/54°C (for medium-rare). Remove from the oven and cover loosely with foil (the temperature will increase as the meat rests) for at least 10 minutes.
4. To serve, cut the meat into slices and serve with the potatoes.

DAUPHINOISE POTATOES

- 2 1/4 cups/560 ml heavy (whipping) cream
- 2 1/4 cups/560 ml milk
- 3 garlic cloves
- 8 large baking potatoes, thinly sliced
- salt and freshly ground pepper to taste
- 4 oz./115 g grated Gruyère cheese

1. Preheat the oven to 375°F/190°C. Generously grease a large gratin dish.
2. In a large saucepan over medium heat, bring the cream, milk, and garlic to simmer. Add the potatoes and cook, stirring gently to prevent sticking, for 3–5 minutes or until just cooked.
3. With a slotted spoon, transfer the potatoes to the prepared dish and then pour over the cream. Discard the garlic. Season with salt and pepper and sprinkle with the cheese.
4. Bake for 30–35 minutes or until the potatoes are tender. Increase the heat for 5 minutes if the top is not brown enough, or put it under the broiler for a few minutes for a crusty topping.

Serves 8

Photo courtesy of Solis Lough Eske Castle

GRILLED RIB EYE WITH COLCANNON POTATO CAKES

WHEN they're in the mood for a steak, diners at Solis Lough Eske Castle, Donegal Town, get to choose not only their cut of beef (an 8 oz./225 g for ladies, 12 oz./350 g for gentlemen) but also the breed (either locally produced Hereford or Angus). The chef serves this 10 oz./300 g rib eye steak with potato cakes that he makes from Colcannon, a traditional dish of mashed potatoes and cabbage or kale. If you like, you can also serve the steak with Gaelic Steak Sauce (recipe follows).

STEAKS

- 2 (10 oz./300 g) rib eye steaks
- olive oil
- sea salt and freshly ground pepper to taste

1. Light a fire in a charcoal grill or preheat a gas grill to medium-high.
2. Season the meat on both sides with olive oil, salt, and pepper. Grill to desired doneness (130°F/54°C for rare, 140°F/60°C for medium, 150°F/65°C for well-done).
3. To serve, put a steak on each plate and top with the potato cake.

GAELIC STEAK SAUCE

- 2 tbsp. unsalted Irish butter
- 2 tbsp. olive oil
- 1 garlic clove, minced
- 1 shallot, minced
- 8 large white mushrooms, chopped
- 1 tsp. Mileeven Honey, or similar brand
- 1/2 tsp. Lakeshore Wholegrain Mustard, or similar brand
- 2 tbsp. Knappogue Castle Single Malt Irish Whiskey
- 3/4 cup/175 ml homemade beef stock or canned low-sodium beef broth
- 3/4 cup/175 ml heavy (whipping) cream
- sea salt and freshly ground pepper
- fresh parsley sprigs for garnish

1. In a large skillet over medium heat, heat the butter and oil. Add the garlic, shallot, and mushroom and cook for 2–3 minutes or until soft but not browned. Stir in the honey and mustard and cook for 1 minute. Add the whiskey and stock or broth and cook for 3–4 minutes or until reduced by half.
2. Whisk in the cream and cook for 2–3 minutes more, or until the sauce thickens. Season to taste with salt and pepper. To serve, spoon some of the sauce over the steak and garnish with the parsley.

Makes about 2 cups

CONTINUED ON NEXT PAGE

COLCANNON POTATO CAKES

- 1 small cabbage, cored, quartered, and shredded
- 2 large baking potatoes, peeled and cut into 1 1/2 inch/3.5 cm pieces
- 3 tbsp. salted Irish butter, cut into small pieces
- 1 small leek (white and green parts), washed and sliced
- 1/2 cup/125 ml milk
- salt and freshly ground pepper to taste
- 1/2 tsp. ground mace
- 2 tbsp. canola oil for frying

1. In separate medium saucepans, cook the cabbage and potatoes in salted boiling water for about 20 minutes or until tender. Drain the cabbage and chop. Drain the potatoes and mash. Combine in a large bowl with the butter.
2. In a small saucepan over medium-low heat, combine the leeks and milk. Cook for 8–10 minutes or until the leeks are tender. Stir into the potato mixture and season with salt, pepper, and mace.
3. Transfer the potato mixture to a large dinner plate and form into a 1/2-inch/1 cm-thick round. With an offset spatula or your fingers, smooth the top. Refrigerate for 10–15 minutes or until potatoes are cold. With a 3 inch/7.5 cm biscuit cutter, cut out 4 rounds.
4. In a large skillet over medium heat, heat the oil. Cook the potato cakes for 3–4 minutes on each side or until browned and heated through.

Makes 4 cakes

Photo courtesy of Magners Irish Cider

BUNRATTY CASTLE CHICKEN WITH MEADE AND APPLE CREAM SAUCE

BUNRATTY Castle is the most authentic and complete medieval fortress in Ireland. Built in the early fifteenth century, the castle was restored in 1954, and later its adjoining Folk Park was developed. One of three castles where the famous, fun-filled medieval banquets take place, Bunratty's banquet is hosted by the Earl of Thomond, who leads singers in an evening of Irish music and song. A four-course meal is served during the entertainment, including this sweet-tart chicken dish with sauce made with Bunratty Meade, Ireland's original honey-wine. Try it with Crushed Potatoes (page 127). Shannon Heritage operates the Bunratty Castle Banquet, which takes place twice nightly year-round.

- 2 tbsp. salted Irish butter, plus more if needed
- 4 (4 oz./115 g) boneless chicken breasts
- salt and freshly ground pepper to taste
- 1 tsp. Lakeshore French Mustard or similar brand
- 1 tsp. Mileeven Irish Honey or similar brand
- 2 tbsp. Bunratty Meade
- 2 medium shallots, peeled and finely chopped
- 1 cooking apple, peeled, cored, and diced
- 1 tbsp. all-purpose flour
- 1/2 cup/125 ml homemade chicken stock or canned low-salt chicken broth
- 1/2 cup/125 ml light cream
- 1 tbsp. fresh lemon juice
- 1 tbsp. chopped fresh flat-leaf parsley for garnish

1. In a large nonstick skillet over medium heat, melt the butter. Season the chicken with salt and pepper and cook on one side for 4–6 minutes or until lightly browned. Using tongs, turn the chicken over and cook for 4–6 minutes longer or until internal temperature reaches 165°F/73°C. Transfer the chicken to a plate, cover, and keep warm.
2. Return the skillet to medium heat and stir in the mustard, honey, and mead, stirring to scrape up the browned bits from the bottom of the pan. Stir in the shallots and apple and cook for 2–3 minutes.
3. Whisk the flour into the pan, cook for 1 minute, and then gradually whisk in the stock. Bring to a boil and cook for 3–5 minutes or until the sauce thickens. Stir in the cream and lemon juice. Reduce the heat and simmer for about 2 minutes longer or until the apple is nearly tender.
4. To serve, put a chicken breast on each of 4 plates and pour the sauce over each. Garnish with parsley and serve with the potatoes.

CONTINUED ON NEXT PAGE

VARIATION: MAGNERS CHICKEN WITH APPLES AND SAGE

THIS easy-to-prepare dish gets a double dose of apple flavor from both tart Granny Smith apples and smooth Magners Irish Cider, produced in Ireland since 1935 from 17 varieties of apples. The sage adds a savory touch, a nice complement to the fruit. The chicken is delicious with Garlic-Herb Mash (page 108).

1. Cook the chicken breasts as above and keep warm.
2. Return the skillet to medium heat and stir in 2 tbsp. chopped shallots, 2 small Granny Smith apples (peeled, cored, and chopped), and 1 tbsp. chopped fresh sage. Cook for about 5 minutes or until the apples are nearly tender.
3. Add 3/4 cup/175 ml Magners Irish Cider and bring to a boil, stirring to scrape up the browned bits from the bottom of the pan. Cook for about 4 minutes or until the sauce is slightly thickened.
4. Reduce the heat, return the chicken to the skillet, and cook, turning once, for about 3 minutes or until heated through.
5. To serve, place a chicken breast in the center of each of 4 plates. Spoon the sauce over the top and serve with the potatoes.

DUCK BREAST WITH CARAMELIZED SHALLOTS AND PORT WINE SAUCE

Like many chefs in Ireland, Noel McMeel, Executive Head Chef at Lough Erne Resort, Enniskillen, Co. Fermanagh, sources as many local ingredients as possible and names the providers on his menu. One of his favorites is fresh duck from Silver Hill, a dedicated and respected breeder of hybrid ducks in Emyvale, Co. Monaghan, but you can use any good natural or organic duck. Serve the duck with Boiled New Potatoes (page 109). Lough Erne Resort is a member of Good Food Ireland.

DUCK

- 4 (4 oz./115 g) boneless duck breasts with skin, trimmed
- 2 tsp. vegetable oil
- 4 shallots, peeled and finely chopped
- 1 stalk celery, chopped
- 1 large carrot, chopped
- 4 tbsp. light brown sugar
- 1 cup/250 ml port
- 1 1/4 cups/300 ml dry red wine
- 1 1/4 cups/300 ml homemade chicken stock or canned low-salt chicken broth

1. Preheat the oven to 400°F/200°C. Score the skin side (cut diagonally about 6 times in each direction to form a diamond pattern; do not cut into the meat). Season with salt and pepper.
2. In a large ovenproof skillet, cook the breasts, skin side up, for 2 minutes and then turn and cook for 5–8 minutes or until the skin begins to crisp but the meat is still pink inside. Turn the breasts over again and cook for 1 minute longer.
3. Drain off any excess fat from the pan and then transfer to the oven and cook the duck for 8–12 minutes (for medium). Remove from the oven and let rest for at least 5 minutes.
4. In a medium skillet over medium heat, heat the oil. Add the shallots, celery, and carrots and cook for 3–4 minutes or until the vegetables are soft and lightly browned. Add the sugar and cook for 2–3 minutes or until the sugar has caramelized the vegetables.
5. Add the port and wine and bring to a boil. Cook for 8–10 minutes or until the liquid is reduced by about 1/3. Add the stock, bring to a boil, and then continue to cook until the sauce thickens and coats the back of a spoon. Strain the sauce into a small saucepan, cover, and keep warm.
6. To serve, cut the duck breast diagonally (against the grain) into 10–12 slices. Serve with the shallots, sauce, and the potatoes.

CONTINUED ON NEXT PAGE

CARAMELIZED SHALLOTS

- 4 tbsp. salted Irish Butter
- 1 lb./450 g shallots, peeled and halved lengthwise
- 1 1/2 cups/350 ml water
- 1 tsp. grated lemon zest
- 1/2 cup/125 ml orange juice
- 1/2 cup/125 ml cider vinegar
- 3 tbsp. light brown sugar
- 1/2 tsp. dried thyme
- 1 bay leaf
- sea salt and freshly ground pepper to taste

1. In a medium saucepan over medium-high heat, melt the butter. Add the shallots and cook, stirring frequently, for about 5 minutes or until lightly browned.
2. Add the water, zest, juice, vinegar, sugar, thyme, bay leaf, salt, and pepper. Bring to a boil and then reduce the heat and simmer for 35–40 minutes or until the shallots are tender when pierced with the tip of a knife and the liquid is syrupy. Cover and keep warm.

Serves 6

FILLET OF SALMON WRAPPED IN BACON AND HERBS

ELLE Isle is a sprawling 470-acre estate located in Lisbellaw, Enniskillen, in the heart of the Fermanagh Lakelands. A favorite of fisherman, walkers, and golfers, the estate is also home to Belle Isle Cookery School, where the emphasis is on fresh, flavorful ingredients. Under the direction of Chef Liz Moore, recipes are inventive enough to impress guests yet simple enough to suit home cooks of all abilities. This lovely salmon dish is just one example of the chef's easy style. Serve this with Crushed Potatoes (recipe follows). Belle Isle Cookery School is a member of Good Food Ireland.

- 10–12 slices streaky rashers or American bacon, plus more if needed
- 2 (1 lb./450 g) fillets of salmon, skinned
- 1 tbsp. Lakeshore French Mustard or similar brand
- salt and freshly ground pepper to taste
- handful of fresh herbs such as flat-leaf parsley, chives, or watercress
- 1 garlic clove
- zest of 1 lemon
- lemon wedges for serving

CRUSHED POTATOES

- 4 large boiling potatoes, unpeeled, cut into 2 inch/5 cm pieces
- 2 tbsp. unsalted Irish butter, cut into pieces
- 2 tbsp. olive oil
- 3 tbsp. crumbled Cashel Blue cheese (optional)
- sea salt and freshly ground pepper to taste

1. Cook the potatoes in salted boiling water for about 15 minutes or until tender. Drain. Return them to the same saucepan to dry out a little.
2. With a wooden spoon, roughly mash the potatoes. Stir in the butter, oil, and cheese (if using). Season with salt and pepper. Reheat just before serving.

Serves 8

1. Put the strips of bacon side by side on a cutting board and run a knife over the top at an angle to lengthen them.
2. Brush both sides of the fish with the mustard, season with salt and pepper, and lay 1 fish fillet, skinned side down, on the bacon. Grate the garlic and lemon zest over the top and cover with the herbs. Lay the remaining fillet on top with the narrow ends matching. Pull the bacon over the fish to wrap.
3. Wet the work surface slightly and lay a large piece of plastic wrap on top. (Wrap should be long and wide enough to wrap the fish several times. Use two sheets together if necessary.) Place the bacon-wrapped salmon near the end of the plastic.
4. Using the wrap as an aid, wrap up the fish as tightly as possible and tie a knot at each end to secure the fish. Refrigerate for 30 minutes (or up to one day).
5. Preheat the oven to 375°F/190°C. Remove the plastic wrap and place the salmon in a shallow ovenproof dish. Roast for 30–35 minutes or until the fish flakes easily with a fork. Remove from the oven and let rest for 10 minutes.
6. To serve, cut the salmon into slices, garnish with lemon, and serve with the potatoes.

Photo courtesy of Doonbeg Lodge

PAN-SEARED SOLE WITH CAPERS, TOMATOES, AND LEMON BUTTER

CHEF Wade Murphy is well known for his light modern dishes "inspired by the ocean." Easy enough for the chef who oversees the kitchen at The Lodge at Doonbeg, Co. Clare—both The Long Room, its fine dining restaurant, and Darby's, its casual eatery pub—situated on the edge of a mile-long stretch of beach on Doughmore Bay. This ocean-inspired dish is one of the most popular on Doonbeg's menu and simple enough for a home cook to make a real impression. Chef Murphy serves it with Boiled New Potatoes (page 109).

- 4 (4 oz./100 g) sole fillets, rinsed and patted dry
- sea salt and freshly ground pepper to taste
- flour for dredging
- 2 tbsp. canola oil
- 4 tbsp. unsalted Irish butter
- 1 tbsp. chopped fresh flat-leaf parsley
- 2 tsp. capers, rinsed under cold water
- 4 cherry tomatoes, cut into quarters
- 1 tbsp. fresh lemon juice
- 10 lemon segments
- 4 lemon wedges

1. Sprinkle both sides of the fish with salt and pepper. Dredge with flour, shaking off excess, and transfer to a plate.
2. In a large skillet over medium-high heat, heat the oil. Add 2 tbsp. of the butter and quickly swirl the pan to coat. When foam subsides, add the fish and cook for 2–3 minutes or until browned.
3. Carefully turn the fish over and cook for 1–2 minutes more or until almost translucent in the center and browned.
4. Divide the fish between 2 warmed plates and tent with aluminum foil. Pour off the cooking juices in the pan and wipe with a paper towel.
5. Return the skillet to the stove over medium-high heat and melt the remaining 2 tbsp. butter. Cook for 1–2 minutes and then remove from the heat and stir in the parsley, lemon juice, capers, tomatoes, and lemon segments.
6. To serve, remove the foil and spoon the sauce over the fish. Garnish with lemon wedges and serve with the potatoes.

SEARED SCALLOPS WITH TOMATO-BUTTER-LEEK SAUCE

S EA scallops, quickly seared and then broiled, are delicious with a flavorful accompaniment like this tomato-butter-leek sauce. This recipe is from Chef John Sheedy, who, with his wife, Martina, operates Sheedy's Country House in Lisdoonvarna, Co. Clare. The hotel, a 300-year-old family home, is the perfect base for touring The Burren, exploring the Cliffs of Moher, or taking in a traditional music set in the village of Doolin. The chef serves it with Champ (page 107).

TOMATO-BUTTER LEEK SAUCE

- 2 tbsp. dry white wine
- 2 tbsp. white wine vinegar
- 2 tbsp. minced shallots
- 1 bay leaf
- freshly ground pepper to taste
- 4 tbsp. heavy (whipping) cream
- 2 leeks (white part only), sliced
- 12 tbsp. unsalted Irish butter, cut into small pieces
- 4 small tomatoes, diced

1. In a small saucepan over medium heat, combine the wine, vinegar, shallots, bay leaf, and pepper. Cook for 8–10 minutes or until reduced by half. Add the cream and leeks and cook for 3–5 minutes or until the leeks are nearly tender.
2. Whisk in the butter, one piece at a time, and stir until smooth. Add the tomatoes and cook for 2–3 minutes or until combined. Set aside and keep warm.

SCALLOPS

- 3 tbsp. unsalted Irish butter
- 1 lb./450 g sea scallops, rinsed and patted dry
- 1 cup/115 g seasoned breadcrumbs
- 1 tbsp. grated lemon zest
- 2–3 leeks (white part only), washed and julienned

1. Preheat the broiler. In a large ovenproof skillet over medium heat, melt 2 tbsp. of the butter. Add the scallops and cook for 2 minutes on each side or until opaque.
2. Sprinkle with the breadcrumbs and lemon zest and place under the broiler 4 inches from the heat source for 2–3 minutes or until the crumbs are lightly browned.
3. In a small saucepan, cook the leeks in salted boiling water for 1–2 minutes or until tender. Drain and add the remaining 1 tbsp. of butter.
4. To serve, divide the leeks among 4 plates. Divide the scallops over the leeks and spoon the sauce over the top.

PAN-FRIED HAKE WITH LEMON AND HERB-BUTTER SAUCE

A close relative to cod, hake is an Atlantic saltwater fish that lends itself to a variety of cooking methods. For the home cook, nothing is as simple as pan-frying, and when you add a handful of fresh herbs and gently cook the fillets in butter, this tasty dish can be on the table in about 15 minutes. You can substitute whiting, haddock, or trout for the hake. Serve it with Crushed Potatoes (page 127) and steamed broccoli.

- 1 tbsp. olive oil
- 4 (6 oz./175 g) hake fillets, skin on and boned, rinsed and patted dry
- salt and freshly ground pepper to taste
- 4 tbsp. salted Irish butter
- 1 tbsp. chopped fresh herbs such as parsley, chives, and tarragon, plus additional for topping
- juice from 1/2 lemon

1. In a large skillet over medium heat, heat the oil. Season the hake with salt and pepper and cook, skin side down, for 1–2 minutes or until the skin begins to crisp. Add 2 tbsp. of the butter and cook for 1–2 minutes longer.
2. Turn the fish over and cook for 3–4 minutes longer or until it flakes easily with a fork. Transfer to warmed plates.
3. Add the remaining 2 tbsp. butter to the skillet and melt over medium heat. Add the herbs and whisk in the lemon juice.
4. To serve, spoon the sauce over the fish and sprinkle with a few grinds of pepper and additional fresh herbs, if desired. Serve with the potatoes and broccoli.

ATLANTIC COD WITH SPINACH, WALNUTS, AND TOMATO CONCASSE

PHILIPP Ferber, Head Chef at Solis Lough Eske Castle, Donegal Town, prefers to use local ingredients in his cooking, and when it comes to seafood, he sources it from nearby Killybegs, one of Ireland's biggest fishing ports. He serves this cod with Garlic-Herb Mash (page 108) and Sautéed Spinach embellished with crushed walnuts (recipe follows).

- 4 (4 oz./100 g) cod fillets, rinsed and patted dry
- sea salt and freshly ground pepper to taste
- 2 tbsp. dry red wine
- 2 tsp. capers, rinsed under cold water
- 1 large tomato, peeled, seeded, and chopped
- 2 lemon slices
- 4 cherry tomatoes for garnish

1. Preheat the oven to 350°F/180°C.
2. Sprinkle both sides of the fish with salt and pepper. In a large skillet over medium heat, heat the oil. Cook the cod, skin side down, for 3–5 minutes or until slightly crisp, and then transfer the pan to the oven and cook for 4–5 minutes more or until almost translucent in the center. Transfer the fish to a warm plate and tent with aluminum foil.

SAUTÉED SPINACH WITH CRUSHED WALNUTS

- 3 tbsp. olive oil
- 3 tbsp. crushed walnuts
- 3 (225 g) bags of baby spinach
- salt and freshly ground pepper to taste

1. In a large skillet over medium heat, heat the oil. Add the walnuts and cook for about 3 minutes or until lightly browned.
2. Stir in the spinach, one bag at a time, and cook, stirring continuously, until the spinach wilts.
3. Repeat with additional bags until heated through.

3. Stir the red wine, capers, diced tomatoes, and lemon into the same skillet and cook for about 3 minutes or until blended.
4. To serve, divide the sauce among 4 serving plates, top with the fish, and garnish with the cherry tomatoes. Serve with the spinach and potatoes.

Photo Courtesy of Lough Eske Castle

CHAPTER No. 5

GRAND FINALES

Breads and cakes are the Irishwoman's true forte: she loves both making them and eating them . . . they are probably the most traditional foods which still exist in Ireland.

THEODORA FITZGIBBON
Irish Traditional Food

Serves 10

GUINNESS TOFFEE PUDDINGS WITH IRISH CREAM SAUCE

THESE "puddings" are a favorite of both the English and the Irish. More like a cake than a pudding, the dessert gets most of its richness from the toffee sauce—this one enhanced with Irish Cream liqueur. For added decadence, Ed Cooney, Executive Chef at The Merrion Hotel (Upper Merrion Street, Dublin), adds Guinness to the date puddings along with raisins and walnuts. It's a favorite at the hotel's Cellar Restaurant, considered one of Dublin's best addresses. Prepare the sauce while the puddings are baking, as they're most delicious when the sauce is poured over the warm little cakes. You can also make them a day ahead, leave the pudding at room temperature, and reheat the sauce in a microwave. The Merrion is a member of Good Food Ireland.

- 1 cup/250 ml Guinness
- 1/2 cup/60 g raisins
- 1/2 cup/60 g walnuts, chopped
- 1/2 cup/60 g dates, chopped
- 1 tbsp. baking soda
- 8 tbsp. unsalted Irish butter, at room temperature
- 3/4 cup/175 g (packed) light brown sugar
- 3 medium eggs
- 2 cups/225 g self-rising flour

IRISH CREAM SAUCE

- 1 cup/250 ml heavy (whipping) cream
- 1 cup/225 g (packed) dark brown sugar
- 4 tbsp. salted Irish butter
- 2 tbsp. Brady's Irish cream liqueur

1. In a medium saucepan over medium heat, combine the cream, brown sugar, and butter. Bring to a boil, and then reduce heat and simmer, without stirring, for 5 minutes or until thickened. Stir in the Irish cream.

Makes about 2 cups

1. In a medium saucepan over medium heat, combine the Guinness, raisins, walnuts, and dates. Bring to a boil and then reduce the heat and simmer for about 5 minutes. Remove from heat, let cool completely, and then stir in the baking soda.
2. Preheat the oven to 325°F/170°C. Generously grease ten 8 oz./250 ml ramekins.
3. In a large bowl, cream the butter and sugar with an electric mixer on medium until light and fluffy. Add the eggs one at a time, and then fold in the flour and date mixture.
4. Spoon the batter into the prepared dishes and bake for 20–25 minutes or until a skewer inserted into the center comes out clean.
5. To serve, remove the puddings from the oven and run a knife around the sides to loosen. Invert the puddings onto serving plates and return to upright. Spoon the toffee sauce over the warm puddings.

MARMALADE PUDDINGS WITH CUSTARD SAUCE

THE Bushmills Inn is a historic coaching inn located in the heart of Northern Ireland's Causeway Coast in the village of Bushmills, Co. Antrim. Local attractions include the famous Giant's Causeway, reputed to be giant Finn McCool's stepping stones to Scotland; seventeenth century Dunluce Castle, headquarters of the McDonnell Clan; and the Old Bushmills Distillery, the oldest working distillery in Ireland. Old-fashioned steamed marmalade puddings like these (recipe adapted) are one of the inn's most popular desserts, especially with rich custard that's best made ahead and allowed to cool before serving.

MARMALADE PUDDINGS

- 8 tbsp. unsalted Irish butter, at room temperature
- 1/2 cup/115 g granulated sugar
- 2 large eggs
- grated zest and juice of 1 orange
- 1 cup/115 g all-purpose flour
- 1 1/2 tsp. baking powder
- 2 tsp. ground allspice
- 6 tbsp. thick-cut orange marmalade
- orange segments and mint sprigs for garnish

1. Preheat the oven to 325°F/170°C. Generously grease six 7 oz./125 ml ramekins.
2. In a medium bowl, cream the butter and sugar with an electric mixer on medium until light and fluffy. Beat in the eggs, orange juice, and zest. Sift in the flour, baking powder, and allspice.
3. Fill each ramekin half full with batter. Divide the marmalade among the ramekins and cover with the remaining batter.
4. Put the dishes in a large baking pan (a large casserole dish with a glass cover is ideal for this) and add enough hot water to the pan to come halfway up the side of the dishes. Cover the pan with plastic wrap (or glass cover) and bake for 55–60 minutes or until the puddings are set and lightly browned. Remove from the oven, uncover, and let cool slightly.
5. To serve, run a knife around the sides of the dishes and turn each pudding out onto a dessert plate. Spoon the custard around the puddings and garnish with orange segments and a sprig of mint.

CUSTARD SAUCE

- 2 cups/500 ml half-and-half
- 5 tbsp. granulated sugar
- 1 vanilla bean (see Note, page 141)
- 5 large egg yolks
- pinch of salt
- 2 tbsp. Bushmills Irish Whiskey

1. In a medium saucepan over medium heat, combine the half-and-half and 2 tbsp. of the sugar.
2. Split the vanilla bean in half, scrape out the seeds, and chop the pod into small pieces. Add to the half-and-half and heat for about 5 minutes or until steaming.
3. In a medium bowl, whisk together the egg yolks, remaining 3 tbsp. sugar, and salt. Gently whisk the half-and-half mixture into the eggs, and then return the custard to the pan and cook, stirring constantly, for 5–8 minutes or until the mixture coats the back of a spoon.
4. Strain the custard into a bowl, stir in the whiskey, and place a piece of plastic wrap directly onto the surface to prevent a skin from forming. Refrigerate for about 4 hours or overnight.

Makes about 2 cups

APPLE-CRANBERRY CRUMBLE

THE Ritz-Carlton Powerscourt, Enniskerry, Co. Wicklow, is set amidst one of the most scenic and historic estates in Ireland. With three restaurants ranging from Gordon Ramsay's fine dining space to McGill's Irish pub, the hotel has food to fit all tastes. This easy but elegant crumble features two autumn fruits, but with a little imagination you can easily substitute what's in season, such as peaches, plums, or pears. Try this with vanilla ice cream or Cinnamon-Mascarpone Whipped Cream (recipe follows).

FILLING

- 4–5 medium Granny Smith apples or a mix of sweet and tart eating apples
- 2 cups/225 g fresh or frozen cranberries
- 5 tbsp. light brown sugar
- 2 tbsp. lemon juice
- 1 vanilla bean, split and scraped (see Note)
- 1 tsp. cinnamon

1. Combine the flour, butter, and sugar in a food processor fitted with a metal blade. Pulse for 15–20 seconds or until soft dough forms. Break up the dough with your fingers to make small pieces and freeze for 1 hour.
2. Preheat the oven to 375°F/190°C. Generously grease an 11x7 inch/28x18 cm baking dish.
3. In large bowl, combine the apples, cranberries, brown sugar, lemon juice, vanilla bean scrapings, and cinnamon. Spoon the fruit mixture into the prepared dish and drop the crumble mix pieces on top. Bake for 30–35 minutes or until the apples are tender and the top is browned. Serve warm with the whipped cream.

CRUMBLE

- 1 1/4 cups/150 g all-purpose flour
- 8 tbsp. salted Irish butter
- 1/3 cup/75 g granulated sugar

CINNAMON-MASCARPONE WHIPPED CREAM

- 1 cup/250 ml heavy (whipping) cream
- 1 cup/250 ml mascarpone cheese
- 1 tsp. vanilla extract
- 2 tbsp. confectioners' sugar

1. In a chilled bowl, combine the cream, mascarpone, vanilla, and confectioners' sugar. Beat with an electric mixer on high until soft peaks form.

NOTE: Vanilla beans, which are actually seed pods, can be found in the baking section of most supermarkets. For maximum flavor, slice the pod down its length and scrape the point of the knife along the inside to release the seeds. Vanilla pods are quite expensive, but the flavor is worth it. After the seeds are scraped out, you can make vanilla sugar by putting the pods into a lidded jar of superfine sugar. Use the sugar in cakes, sauces, and other desserts. You can continue to add used pods and replace with more sugar as needed.

Makes about 2 cups

Photo courtesy of Lily O'Brien's Chocolate Café

LILY O'BRIEN'S CHOCOLATE BREAD AND BUTTER PUDDING

MARY Anne O'Brien is the woman behind Lily O'Brien's, one of Ireland's most successful chocolate companies. With little more than two saucepans, a wooden spoon, and her then toddler, Lily, acting as production manager, Mary Ann began to create high quality chocolate recipes for friends and family in the kitchen of her Kildare home. O'Brien eventually formed a mini chocolate-making enterprise in 1992 and named the company for her daughter. Now based in Newbridge, Co. Kildare, her wide range of chocolates is available throughout Ireland, the U.K. and parts of Europe, including dark baking chocolate used in this contemporary bread pudding. The first-ever Lily O'Brien's Chocolate Café, a cozy yet cosmopolitan coffee house, opened in New York (36 West 40th Street at Bryant Park) in March 2009.

- 10–12 slices stale white bread, crusts removed, cut into triangles
- 5 oz./115 g Lily O'Brien's Pure Dark Baking Chocolate
- 5 tbsp. unsalted Irish butter
- 1/2 cup/115 g granulated sugar
- 2 1/4 cups/560 ml heavy (whipping) cream
- 4 large eggs
- crème fraîche for serving
- brown sugar for sprinkling

1. Lightly grease a gratin dish. Arrange the bread triangles in the dish with the slices overlapping slightly. Set aside.
2. In a heatproof bowl, microwave the chocolate, butter, sugar, and cream on high for 2 minutes. Stir until smooth and then cool to lukewarm.
3. In a medium bowl, beat the eggs and then whisk into the chocolate mixture until smooth. Pour over the bread, pressing down with a spoon to ensure that the slices are covered. Cover and refrigerate for at least 12 hours.
4. Preheat the oven to 400°F/200°C. Place the baking dish in a large baking pan. Add enough hot water to come halfway up the sides of the dish. Bake for 50–60 minutes or until the pudding is set and the top is firm. Remove the baking dish from the water and let cool on a wire rack.
5. To serve, spoon the pudding onto dessert plates, top with a spoonful of crème fraîche, and sprinkle with some brown sugar.

APPLE-ALMOND TARTS

BELFAST'S Merchant Hotel (16 Skipper Street), in the heart of the city's historic cathedral district, was the original headquarters of the Ulster Bank and one of the city's most architecturally important buildings. Showcasing a blend of High Victorian grandeur and Art Deco chic, the hotel is also a hub of culinary style with The Great Room for fine dining, The Cloth Ear for casual comfort food, two bars, and a nightclub. Like many Ulster cooks, Executive Chef Tony O'Neill fancies local ingredients—seafood from Strangford and Carlingford Loughs, Glenarm lamb, Portavogie prawns, Dundrum oysters, and apples from Armagh or Portadown that he uses in these frangipane tarts (adapted here). The Merchant Hotel is a member of Good Food Ireland.

FILLING

- 8 tbsp. salted Irish butter, at room temperature
- 1/2 cup/115 g plus 1 tbsp. superfine sugar
- 2 large eggs
- 1 cup/115 g almonds, ground
- 1 tbsp. finely chopped lemon zest
- 2 eating apples, peeled, cored, and diced
- 1 tbsp. salted Irish butter, melted
- superfine sugar for dusting
- 2–3 tbsp. warmed apricot jam for glazing
- clotted cream for serving

PASTRY

- 1 3/4 cups/200 g sifted all-purpose flour, plus extra for dusting
- pinch of salt
- 3 tbsp. granulated sugar
- 8 tbsp. unsalted Irish butter, cut into small pieces
- 3 egg yolks
- 1 1/2 tbsp. ice water

1. Combine the flour, salt, sugar, and butter in a food processor and pulse 5–8 times or until the mixture resembles coarse crumbs. Add the yolks and water and process until the mixture forms soft dough.
2. Transfer the dough to a lightly floured surface, and with floured hands form into a ball. Wrap in plastic and chill for 30 minutes.
3. Preheat the oven to 350°F/180°C. Generously grease six 4 inch/10 cm tartlet pans and dust with flour.
4. 4. Roll out the pastry to a 1/2 inch/1 cm thick round. Using a 6 inch/15 cm plate or saucer as a guide, cut out 6 rounds. Transfer each round to the prepared pans and fold in the excess to form thick edges. Cover with foil and half-fill with pie weights or dried beans. Bake for 10 minutes, remove the foil, and bake for 5 minutes more or until lightly browned. Remove from the oven and let cool for about 15 minutes.
5. To make the filling, in a large bowl, cream the butter and sugar with an electric mixer on medium until light and fluffy. Beat in the eggs one at a time. Fold in the almonds and lemon zest and spoon into the pastry shells.
6. Arrange the apples over the top and gently push down into the filling. Brush the tops of the apples with the melted butter and dust with the remaining sugar. Bake for 40–45 minutes or until the filling is puffed and golden and the apples nearly tender.
7. Turn off the oven and brush the top of each tart with the apricot jam. Leave the tarts in the oven with the door ajar for 15 minutes.
8. To serve, remove the tarts from the oven and serve warm with the cream.

KERRY APPLE CAKE

THIS is one of my all-time favorite cakes, possibly because my ancestors hailed from the Kingdom of Kerry or simply because it's so easy to make and delicious to eat. Chef Mark Johnston of the luxurious Park Hotel Kenmare, Co. Kerry, says this cake is "standard fare" on his menu throughout the year, and legendary Irish cook Myrtle Allen of Ballymaloe House, Co. Cork, says, "Homemade apple cakes are the most popular sweet in Ireland." Serve it with whipped cream or vanilla ice cream. The Park Kenmare is a member of Good Food Ireland.

- 12 tbsp. unsalted Irish butter, at room temperature
- 3/4 cup/175 g granulated sugar
- 2 large eggs, beaten
- 2 cups/225 g self-rising flour
- 2 medium cooking apples, peeled, cored, and diced
- 1 tsp. lemon zest
- 2 tbsp. Demerara (crystallized cane) sugar
- pinch of ground cinnamon
- pinch of ground nutmeg
- whipped cream or vanilla ice cream for serving

1. Preheat the oven to 350°F/180°C. Generously grease a 9 inch/22.5 cm loaf pan and line with wax paper.
2. In a large bowl, beat the butter and sugar with an electric mixer on medium until light and fluffy. Gradually beat in the eggs and flour. Stir in the apples and lemon rind. Transfer the batter to the prepared pan, smooth the top, and then sprinkle with the Demerara sugar, cinnamon, and nutmeg.
3. Bake for 50–55 minutes or until a skewer inserted into the center comes out clean. Remove from the oven and let cool on a wire rack for about 10 minutes before cutting the cake into slices.

Serves 8–10

CREAM CHEESE POUND CAKE WITH CIDER-POACHED PEARS

The name "pound cake" comes from the rather precise recipe for a cake that calls for 1 pound of sugar, 1 pound of butter, and 1 pound of flour. Some additional flavoring, such as nutmeg, lemon juice, or vanilla, is often added. Today the ratio of sugar to butter to flour sometimes varies, but the results are usually the same. Pound cake is one of those reliable cakes that every culture seems to embrace because it goes well with everything. Try it with pears poached in Magners Pear Cider, a new flavor from the renowned Irish cider company, or some fresh berries. Serve it with plain whipped cream or flavor it with a few tablespoons of the poaching liquid.

- 1 (8 oz./225 g) package unsalted Irish butter, at room temperature
- 1 (8 oz./225 g) package cream cheese, at room temperature
- 2 cups/450 g granulated sugar
- 2 tsp. vanilla extract
- 2 1/4 cups/250 g self-rising cake flour
- 6 large eggs

1. Preheat the oven to 350°F/180°C. Butter a 10 inch/25 cm tube pan and line with wax paper.
2. In a large bowl, beat the butter and cream cheese with an electric mixer on medium until light and fluffy. Add the sugar, vanilla, and flour and beat on medium-low for 2–3 minutes or until blended. Add the eggs, one at a time, beating well after each addition.
3. Pour the batter into the prepared pan and bake for about 50 minutes or until a skewer inserted into the center comes out clean.
4. Remove the cake from the oven and let it cool on a wire rack for 15 minutes. Invert the pan onto a plate, remove the cake, and then return the cake to upright and let cool completely before cutting into slices.
5. To serve, put some pear slices next to each piece of cake and top with whipped cream, if desired.

CIDER-POACHED PEARS

- 1 cup/225 g granulated sugar
- 3/4 cup/175 ml Magners Pear Cider
- 3/4 cup/175 ml dry white wine
- 1 tsp. grated lemon zest
- 1 stick cinnamon
- 4 medium pears, peeled

1. In a medium saucepan over medium heat, bring the sugar, cider, white wine, zest, and cinnamon to a boil. Add the pears, reduce heat to medium, and cook, covered, for 15–20 minutes or until tender. Cool pears in poaching liquid and then cut in half, core, and slice.

Photo courtesy of Bewleys Café

CARROT CAKE WITH CREAM CHEESE ICING

NEARLY every tea shop, coffee house, pub, and fine dining restaurant in Ireland serves some variation of carrot cake, a dessert thought to have evolved from a medieval carrot pudding. The cake gained popularity in the 1960s and is now a staple in Irish, English, and American cuisine. This recipe is one of the most popular desserts at Bewley's Grafton Street Café, a Dublin institution since 1927, when Ernest Bewley opened the restaurant and modeled it after the great European cafés of Paris and Vienna. The cream cheese icing is nearly obligatory, and if you wish, you can add a tablespoon of Mileeven Irish Honey!

- 2 cups/225 g all-purpose flour
- 1 1/2 tsp. baking powder
- 1 1/2 tsp. baking soda
- 1 tsp. salt
- 1 1/2 tsp. ground cinnamon
- 4 large eggs
- 1 1/2 cups/350 g granulated sugar
- 1/2 cup/125 ml sunflower oil
- 3 cups/250 g grated carrots
- 1/4 cup/30 g chopped walnuts

ICING

- 1 (8 oz./225 g) package cream cheese, at room temperature
- 4 cups/225 g confectioners' sugar
- 8 tbsp. unsalted Irish butter, at room temperature
- 1 tsp. vanilla extract

1. In a large bowl, beat the cream cheese, sugar, butter, and vanilla with an electric mixer on medium until smooth.

1. Preheat the oven to 350°F/180°C. Generously butter two 9 inch/22.5 cm round baking pans.
2. In a medium bowl, sift together the flour, baking powder, baking soda, salt, and cinnamon. Set aside.
3. In a large bowl, beat the eggs and sugar with an electric mixer on medium until light and fluffy. Slowly beat in the oil. Stir into the flour mixture and then stir in the carrots and walnuts.
4. Transfer the batter to the prepared pans and bake for 45–50 minutes or until a skewer inserted into the center comes out clean. Remove from the oven and let cool completely on a wire rack.
5. Spread the icing between the layers and on the sides and top of the cake. Refrigerate until the frosting is firm and then cut into slices.

OATMEAL-STOUT CAKE WITH BROWN BREAD ICE CREAM

THE origin of this cake is mysterious at best. It appears to go by a variety of names, but the ingredients are generally the same whether it's called Scots-Irish Cake, Oatmeal Cake, or Brown Sugar-Oatmeal Cake. This recipe is a delicious interpretation from Chef Philipp Ferber of Solis Lough Eske Castle, Donegal Town, who tops it with rich Brown Bread Ice Cream. Chef Ferber makes the ice cream himself, but you can purchase premium vanilla ice cream and add your own brown soda breadcrumbs. Make the ice cream a few hours or up to one day ahead of when you plan to serve this cake.

- 1 cup/115 g McCann's Irish oatmeal
- 1 1/4 cups/300 ml Guinness
- 2 cups/225 g all-purpose flour
- 1 tsp. baking soda
- 1/2 tsp. salt
- 1 tsp. Mixed Spice (page 33)
- 1/2 tsp. ground cinnamon
- 8 tbsp. unsalted Irish butter, at room temperature
- 1 cup/200 g Demerara (crystallized cane) sugar
- 1 cup/200 g (packed) dark brown sugar
- 2 large eggs
- 1 tsp. vanilla extract
- 1/2 tsp. orange zest
- 1/2 tsp. lemon zest

TOPPING

- 6 tbsp. unsalted Irish butter
- 1/2 cup/150 g (packed) light brown sugar
- 2/3 cup/150 ml sweetened condensed milk
- 1 cup/115 g McCann's Irish oatmeal
- 4 tbsp. sliced almonds, toasted

1. In a medium saucepan over medium heat, combine the butter, sugar, and milk. Bring slowly to a boil and cook for 2–3 minutes or until smooth.
2. Remove from the heat and stir in the oatmeal and almonds.

1. In a medium bowl, combine the oatmeal and Guinness. Let soak for about 1 hour.
2. Preheat the oven to 325°F/170°C. Generously grease a 9 inch/22.5 cm springform pan.
3. In a large bowl, sift together the flour, baking soda, salt, Mixed Spice, and cinnamon.
4. In a medium bowl, cream the butter and sugars with an electric mixer on medium until light and fluffy. Add the eggs, one at a time, and then stir in the vanilla, orange, and lemon zest. Fold in the flour mixture, and then stir in the oatmeal mixture.
5. Transfer the batter to the prepared pan and bake for 35–40 minutes or until a toothpick inserted into the center comes out clean. Remove from the oven and transfer to a wire rack. Pour the topping over the cake and let cool. Refrigerate for 1–2 hours or until the topping is set.
6. To serve, remove the side of the pan and then cut the cake into slices. Serve warm with the ice cream.

CONTINUED ON NEXT PAGE

BROWN BREAD ICE CREAM

- 2 cups/450 g homemade brown soda breadcrumbs (page 41)
- 2 tbsp. light brown sugar
- 1 pint/450 g premium vanilla ice cream, slightly softened

1. Preheat the oven to 375°F/190°C.
2. In a medium bowl toss the breadcrumbs with the brown sugar. Spread the breadcrumbs out onto a baking sheet and toast them for about 15 minutes or until crisp and browned. Remove from the oven and let cool.
3. Turn the ice cream out into a large bowl. Stir in the breadcrumbs and then return the ice cream mixture to a plastic container and freeze for at least 30 minutes or until firm.

LILY'S CHOCOLATE ROULADE WITH RASPBERRY CREAM

In addition to the line of gourmet chocolates with luscious fillings like crème brûlée, hazelnut torte, honeycomb crisp, and lemon meringue pie, Lily O'Brien's (see page 143), also makes pure dark baking chocolate for use in recipes like this roulade. The first-ever Lily O'Brien's Chocolate Café, where you receive a premium chocolate with every cup of coffee, opened in midtown Manhattan (36 West 40th Street at Bryant Park) in 2009.

- 2/3 cup/150 g Lily O'Brien's Pure Dark Baking Chocolate
- 5 large eggs, separated
- 1 cup/225 g sugar
- 1 cup/250 ml heavy (whipping) cream
- 1 cup/175 g raspberries, plus more for serving
- confectioners' sugar for dusting

1. Preheat the oven to 350°F/180°C. Line a 15x10-inch/37.5x25 cm jelly roll (Swiss roll) pan with buttered aluminum foil or wax paper.
2. In a heatproof bowl, microwave the chocolate on high for 1 minute. Stir, and then microwave for 30–45 seconds longer or until almost melted. Let cool for about 5 minutes.
3. In a medium bowl, beat the egg yolks and sugar with an electric mixer on medium until thick and lemon colored. Stir into the chocolate.
4. In a clean dry bowl, beat the egg whites with an electric mixer on high until soft peaks form. Fold into the chocolate mixture and then transfer the batter to the prepared pan. With a spatula, smooth to the edges. Bake for 12–15 minutes or until set.
5. Remove from the oven and let cool for 5 minutes. Run a sharp knife around the cake to loosen it from the pan. Invert the cake onto a lint-free kitchen towel dusted with confectioners' sugar and then peel off the foil or paper. Starting at the short end, roll up the cake with the towel, jellyroll fashion. Cool completely.
6. In a small bowl, whip the cream with an electric mixer on high until stiff peaks form. Unroll the cake, spread with the whipped cream to edges on each side, and scatter the raspberries onto the cream. Reroll and place seam side down on a serving plate.
7. To serve, cut the roulade into slices, dust with confectioners' sugar, and serve with additional raspberries, if desired.

Photo courtesy of Castle Brands

IRISH COFFEE MERINGUES

IRISH Coffee is one of the country's most iconic beverages (recipe page 167), and because of its distinctive flavors—coffee, whiskey, sugar, and cream—it lends itself as an ingredient in all types of recipes, especially desserts. This chilled version from the Brooks Hotel (Drury Street, Dublin), has all the classic components but with the crunchy addition of walnuts and crumbled meringues. Brooks Hotel is a member of Good Food Ireland.

- 2 large egg whites, at room temperature
- 1/2 cup/115 g superfine sugar
- 1 tsp. corn starch
- 2 tbsp. finely chopped walnuts
- 1 cup/250 ml freshly whipped cream
- 1 cup/250 ml hot coffee
- 2 tbsp. Knappogue Castle Single Malt Irish Whiskey
- 2 tbsp. Demerara (crystallized cane) sugar
- shaved chocolate for topping (optional)

1. Preheat the oven to 350°F/180°C. Line a baking sheet with parchment paper.
2. In a clean dry bowl, beat the egg whites with an electric mixer on high until stiff peaks form. Slowly add the sugar (it can be warmed in the microwave to speed up the process and produce a better mix) and cornstarch and continue beating until the mixture is smooth and glossy. Fold in the walnuts.
3. Spoon the meringue onto the prepared pan in 4 even mounds, spacing apart. Reduce the oven temperature to 250°F/130°C and bake for about 1 hour or until the meringues are dry. Turn off the oven and leave the meringues for 1 hour longer.
4. While the meringues are cooking, combine the coffee, whiskey, and sugar. Stir to dissolve the sugar and then refrigerate until cold.
5. To serve, crumble the meringues into a medium bowl and fold in the whipped cream. Divide the Irish Coffee into 4 martini glasses and spoon the meringue mix on top. Garnish with some shaved chocolate, if desired.

LILY'S LAVA CAKES WITH IRISH COFFEE SAUCE

A favorite in all chocolate-loving nations, these little cakes score bonus points when they're made with Lily O'Brien's pure dark baking chocolate and served on Irish coffee-flavored custard. Make the sauce a few hours or up to one day ahead of when you plan to serve this dessert.

- 2/3 cup/150 g Lily O'Brien's Pure Dark Baking Chocolate
- 8 tbsp. unsalted Irish butter
- 4 large eggs
- 1 cup/225 g granulated sugar
- 1 cup/115 g all-purpose flour
- confectioners' sugar for dusting
- whipped cream for serving
- fresh berries for serving

1. Preheat the oven to 350°F/180°C. Spray eight 4 oz./125 ml ramekins with cooking oil spray with four.
2. In a heatproof bowl, microwave the chocolate and butter on high for 2 minutes. Stir until smooth and then cool to lukewarm.
3. In a medium bowl, beat the eggs and sugar with an electric mixer on medium until light and fluffy. Stir in the flour and chocolate mixture. Transfer the batter to the prepared dishes and bake for 10-12 minutes, or until the tops are firm.
4. To serve, divide the coffee sauce among 8 dessert plates. Run a knife around the edges of the dishes, invert them onto dessert plates, and then return to upright and place on top of the sauce. Dust with confectioners' sugar and serve immediately with whipped cream and berries.

IRISH COFFEE SAUCE

- 6 large egg yolks
- 1/2 cup/115 g granulated sugar
- 1 1/2 cups /350 ml half-and-half
- 1 tsp. instant espresso powder
- 2 tsp. Knappogue Castle Single Malt Irish Whiskey

1. In a medium bowl, whisk together the egg yolks and sugar until well blended.
2. In a medium saucepan over medium heat, heat the half-and-half for about 5 minutes or until steaming. Gradually whisk the half-and-half into the egg yolk mixture, return to the saucepan, and stir in the espresso powder.
3. Cook over medium-low heat for 4–5 minutes or until the custard thickens and coats the back of a spoon. Transfer the sauce to a bowl and place a piece of plastic wrap directly onto the surface to prevent a skin from forming. Refrigerate for about 4 hours or overnight.

Makes 2 cups

KNAPPOGUE CASTLE LEMON CHEESECAKE

In 1467, Sean MacNamara built Knappogue Castle, a brilliant example of a medieval tower house, near the village of Quin, Co. Clare. Through the next several centuries, various renovations of the castle took place, but during the 1920s it fell into complete disrepair. The Andrews family of Texas eventually purchased it in 1966, restored it to its fifteenth century glory, and began bottling vintage Irish whiskey under the Knappogue Castle name. Shannon Heritage later added the property as a venue for its medieval banquets. A four-course meal is served during the entertainment, ending with "rastin," a lemony cheesecake similar to this recipe. The Knappogue Castle Banquet is held from April to October.

FILLING

- 1 (1/3 oz./8.5 g) package lemon-flavored gelatin
- 1 cup/250 ml boiling water
- 1 (8 oz./225 g) package cream cheese, at room temperature
- 1 cup/225 g granulated sugar
- zest of 2 lemons
- juice of 1 lemon
- 1 cup/250 ml heavy (whipping) cream
- 1 (8 oz./250 ml) container plain yogurt
- fresh berries for serving (optional)

CRUST

- 8 tbsp. salted Irish Butter, melted
- 3 cups/350 g digestive biscuits or graham cracker crumbs
- 2 tbsp. granulated sugar

1. In a medium bowl, combine the butter, biscuit crumbs, and sugar. Press the mixture into the bottom and up the sides of a 10 inch/25 cm springform pan. Refrigerate for about 30 minutes to firm the crust.
2. In a small bowl, dissolve the gelatin in the water. Let cool until thick but not set.
3. In a large bowl, beat the cream cheese, sugar, lemon zest, and lemon juice with an electric mixer on high until smooth. Set aside.
4. In a medium bowl, whip the cream with an electric mixer on high until stiff peaks form. Pour in the gelatin mixture and continue to mix until well blended. Fold in the yogurt and then fold in the cream cheese mixture. Pour over the crust, cover, and refrigerate overnight or until set.
5. To serve, release the side of the pan and cut the cake into slices. Top with fresh berries, if desired.

CONTINUED ON NEXT PAGE

VARIATIONS:

CROSSOGUE IRISH COFFEE CURD CHEESECAKE

As a way to use up the produce from her garden, Veronica Molloy began making preserves at her home in Ballycahill, near Thurles, Co. Tipperary, and selling them at local country markets. She currently makes more than 80 varieties of fruit preserves as well as curds, like the whiskey-coffee flavored one for this cheesecake.

Prepare the biscuit crust as above. Substitute 1 (1/4 oz./7 g) package unflavored gelatin for the lemon gelatin and dissolve in boiling water with 5 tbsp. sugar. Omit the lemon juice and zest. In a large bowl, beat 1 (8 oz./225 g) package cream cheese (at room temperature) until smooth. Whip 1 cup/225 g heavy (whipping) cream until stiff peaks form. Fold in 1 (8 oz./225 g) jar Crossogue Irish coffee curd and 1 (8 oz./225 g) container plain yogurt or mascarpone cheese. Slowly beat in the gelatin mixture and then pour over the crust. Chill until set.

MAGNERS CIDER AND APPLE CHEESECAKE

Tracy Horgan, Pastry Chef at the Killarney Park Hotel, Town Center, Killarney, Co. Kerry, makes a tart-sweet cheesecake flavored with apple purée, Magners Irish Cider, and Sour Apple Pucker (imitation Schnapps liqueur). For more apple power, she tops the cheesecake with a cider jelly glaze.

Prepare the biscuit crust as above. In a small saucepan over medium heat, cook 2 Granny Smith apples (peeled, cored, and chopped), 2 tbsp. granulated sugar, and 1 tbsp. Sour Apple Pucker for about 10 minutes or until the apples are soft. Purée the apples in a food processor or blender, return to a small bowl, and stir in 1 (1/4 oz./7 g) package unflavored gelatin. In a large bowl, beat 1 (8 oz./225 g) package cream cheese (at room temperature), 1 cup/225 g heavy (whipping) cream, and 1 cup/115 g confectioners' sugar with an electric mixer on medium until smooth. Slowly beat in the gelatin mixture and then pour over the crust. Chill until set. In a small saucepan over medium heat, heat 1 cup/250 ml Magners Irish Cider. Stir in 1 (1/4 oz./7 g) package unflavored gelatin. Let cool and then pour over the cheesecake and return to refrigerator until glaze is set. Killarney Park Hotel is a member of Good Food Ireland.

Photo courtesy of Lough Erne Resort

LOUGH ERNE WHITE CHOCOLATE AND BAILEY'S PARFAITS

At Lough Erne Resort, Enniskillen, Co. Fermanagh, Executive Chef Noel McMeel is known for both his eclectic and traditional dishes. Here he defers to tradition with a blend of Bailey's Irish cream, white chocolate, and whipped cream for an ice cream-like "parfait." The chef freezes the mixture in molds, but you can freeze it in a plastic container and serve it in martini or parfait glasses.

- 1 1/4 cups/300 g granulated sugar
- 1/2 cup/125 ml water
- 7 large egg yolks
- 8 oz./225 g white chocolate, melted
- 1 3/4 cups/450 ml heavy (whipping) cream,
- 1/4 cup/50 ml Bailey's Irish cream
- whipped cream for topping
- shaved chocolate for topping

1. In a medium saucepan over medium heat, bring the sugar and water to a boil. Continue to boil until the mixture is syrupy and reaches 225°F/110°C on a candy thermometer.
2. Beat the egg yolks with an electric mixer on medium until pale and frothy. Gradually beat the syrup into the egg yolks and then slowly whisk in the white chocolate. Let cool.
3. Whip the cream with an electric mixer on high until stiff peaks form. Fold the whipped cream and Bailey's into the white chocolate mixture and transfer to a plastic container. Freeze for 2–3 hours or until nearly firm.
4. To serve, spoon into 8 parfait or martini glasses and top with whipped cream and shaved chocolate.

CHRISTMAS PUDDING WITH BRANDY BUTTER

"NOTHING says Christmas more to me than my mother-in-law's Christmas pudding," so says Cathal Kavanagh, Head Chef at Carton House, Maynooth, Co. Kildare. Handed down from one generation to the next, this treat is to Kavanagh "undoubtedly the best homemade pudding I have ever tasted." Thankfully, he's willing to share the sacred recipe and is delighted that readers might opt to cook their own pudding and not resort to a "shop bought version." Brandy butter is the traditional topping for Christmas pudding and it's also delicious with holiday mince pies and tarts.

- 4 tbsp. sultanas (golden raisins), chopped
- 1/2 cup/60 g raisins, chopped
- 1/2 cup/60 g currants, chopped
- 4 tbsp. candied mixed peel, chopped
- 1 Granny Smith apple, peeled, cored, and grated
- 2 tbsp. chopped almonds
- 1/2 cup/60 g all-purpose flour
- 1 cup/115 g breadcrumbs
- 2 large eggs, beaten
- 2 tbsp. Knappogue Castle Single Malt Irish whiskey
- juice and zest of half an orange
- 8 tbsp. salted Irish butter
- 1/2 cup/115 g (packed) light brown sugar
- 1/2 tsp. mixed spice (page 33)
- 1/4 tsp. salt

1. In a large bowl, combine the sultanas, raisins, currants, mixed peel, apple, and almonds. Stir in the flour and breadcrumbs and mix well. Stir in the eggs, whiskey, orange juice, and zest.
2. In a medium bowl, beat the sugar and eggs with an electric mixer on medium until light and fluffy. Stir in the mixed spice and salt, and then stir into the fruit mix. Cover and refrigerate overnight.
3. Grease a pudding mold or deep, heatproof bowl. Transfer the pudding mixture to the mold and cover the surface directly with a round of greased wax paper or parchment paper. Cover with a tight-fitting lid or with another piece of parchment paper or aluminum foil a few inches larger than the bowl. Tie it with kitchen string.
4. Put a rack in the bottom of a large saucepan, put the pudding on top, and pour in enough hot water to come 1/3 of the way up the side. Cover the pan and steam over low heat for about 6 hours or until the pudding is firm. Replace water as necessary.
5. Remove the pudding from the pan and let cool completely. Wrap in foil and store in a cool, dry place for up to 6 weeks.
6. Return the pudding to the mold or bowl and reheat (as above) for about 2 hours or until heated through. To serve, invert the pudding onto a hot plate, pour a little whiskey over the top, and ignite just before serving. Cut into slices and serve with the Brandy Butter.

BRANDY BUTTER

- 8 tbsp. unsalted Irish butter, at room temperature
- 1 1/4 cups/175 g confectioners' sugar, sifted
- 2 tbsp. fresh lemon juice
- 1 cup/250 ml brandy

1. Cream the butter and the sugar with an electric mixer on medium until light and fluffy. Gradually beat in the lemon juice and brandy. Spoon into a bowl, cover, and refrigerate.

Irish Coffee and Other Drinks

Irish Coffee

In 1943, chef-barman Joe Sheridan decided that a blend of cream, hot coffee, and Irish whiskey would make a perfect welcoming drink for cold and weary passengers arriving at the town of Foynes, Co. Limerick, from the United States on the "flying boats, the first transatlantic passenger planes." He wanted the drink to be warm and welcoming, Irish in character, and sophisticated enough to appeal to international travelers. After many experiments over a number of years, including the addition of sugar, Sheridan finally came up with the recipe for what would become the quintessential Irish drink. When Shannon International Airport opened in 1947, Irish coffee became its official beverage.

Joe Sheridan's original recipe is as follows: Heat a stemmed, heatproof goblet by running it under very hot water. Pour in 1 jigger Irish whiskey (Knappogue Castle Single Malt preferred). Add 3 cubes of sugar and fill the goblet with strong black coffee to within 1 inch of the rim. Stir to dissolve the sugar. Top off with lightly whipped cream. Do not stir after adding the cream, as the true flavor is obtained by drinking the hot mixture through the cream. Sláinte!

Leopold Bloom
Makes 1 cocktail

- 1 1/4 oz. Knappogue Castle Single Malt Irish Whiskey
- 1 1/4 oz. Festival pale cream sherry
- 1/4 oz. Cointreau liqueur
- 1 tsp. St-Germain elderflower liqueur
- dash of bitters

1. Combine all the ingredients in a shaker and pour over ice into a brandy glass.
2. Garnish with a lemon twist.

The Knapster
Makes 1 cocktail

- 2 oz. Knappogue Castle Single Malt Irish Whiskey
- 3/4 oz. Dubonnet Rouge
- 3/4 oz. lemon juice

1. Combine all the ingredients in a shaker filled with ice.
2. Strain into a martini glass and garnish with a lemon twist.

CASTLE TO CASTLE
Makes 1 cocktail

- 1 1/4 ounces Knappogue Castle Single Malt Whiskey
- 2 oz. whiskey sour mix
- club soda to taste
- orange slice for garnish

1. Combine the whiskey and sour mix in a shaker filled with ice.
2. Pour into a tumbler, add club soda, and garnish with an orange slice.

An Irish Cheese Board

During the late 1970s, a few enterprising dairy farmers began a natural revival of farmhouse cheese making in Ireland on land that had been farmed by the same families for generations and on small properties bought by people who wanted to escape to the peace of the Irish countryside. The first cheeses were made to satisfy the desire for more interesting food than was then available, and later ones were developed by European expats who had moved to Ireland and missed their native cheeses.

With dozens of farmhouse cheeses being crafted in Ireland today—along with others made by dairy cooperatives like Kerrygold—a cheese board is the best way to present them in all their glorious variety both before and after dinner.

A general rule is to offer at least one or two artisanal cheeses from each of the major categories: a soft or semi-soft cheese like Ardrahan, Ballybrie, Carrigbyrne, Cooleeney, St. Killian, Durrus, Dunbarra, Gubbeen, or Milleens; a semi-firm cheese like Carrigaline, Coolea, Knockdrinna, or Knockanore; a blue-veined cheese like Ballyblue, Bellingham, Cashel Blue, or Crozier Blue; a goat's or sheep cheese like Ardsallagh, Corleggy, Knockalara, Cratloe Hills, or St. Tola; and a well-aged hard cheese like Desmond or Gabriel.

Cahill's Farms makes interesting cheeses flavored with Guinness or Kilbeggan whiskey, as well as two speckled with herbs or chives. Most of these are available only in specialty markets or from online sources, but Kerrygold's Dubliner, Blarney Castle, Swiss, Aged and Reserved Cheddars, and Ivernia are widely available in the U.S., as well as Duhallow, a specialty cheese from the makers of Ardrahan.

Provide at least 2 ounces of cheese per person on a cheese board. Cut cheeses for each portion while cold, but bring to room temperature before serving. Arrange generous wedges of cheese on a large plate, wooden board, or piece of marble and provide several knives: a wide blade for semi-firm cheeses like Coolea, a curved spreader for soft-ripened cheeses like Milleens, a thin blade for semi-soft cheeses like Gubbeen, a heart-shaped blade for hard cheeses like Gabriel, a cheese wire for cutting blues so they don't crumble, and a forked cheese knife for picking up precut pieces.

Serve Boilie goat's cheese "pearls" (little balls of cheese marinated in sunflower oil and herbs) with toothpicks, and surround cheeses with fresh and dried fruits and Irish honey for drizzling. Offer a variety of breads, crackers, oatcakes (look for plain and smoked oatcakes from Ditty's, a renown Ulster artisan bakery), nuts (try the Candied Pecans on page 173), Mileeven Irish Honey (for drizzling on hard cheeses), and chutneys such as Pear-Dried Cranberry Chutney (page 59) or one of these:

CONTINUED ON NEXT PAGE

APPLE-PEAR CHUTNEY
Makes 1 1/2 cups / 350 ml

- 1 shallot, finely chopped
- 5 tbsp. cider vinegar
- 1 tsp. minced fresh ginger
- 1 cup/225 g (packed) light brown sugar
- 3/4 cup/175 g sultanas (golden raisins)
- 1 tart apple, peeled, cored, and diced
- 1 firm ripe pear, peeled, cored, and diced

1. In a large saucepan over medium heat, combine all the ingredients. Bring to a boil and then reduce heat and simmer, uncovered, for 20–25 minutes or until the mixture thickens.
2. Remove from the heat and let cool to room temperature.
3. Cover and refrigerate for up to 2 weeks. Serve at room temperature.

CRANBERRY-WALNUT CHUTNEY
Makes 2 cups / 500 ml

- 1 1/2 cups/175 g cranberries
- 2/3 cup/150 g (packed) light brown sugar
- 1/2 cup/60 g chopped dates
- 1 celery stalk, chopped
- 1 tart apple, peeled, cored, and diced
- 1 tbsp. chopped candied ginger
- 1 tbsp. fresh lemon juice
- 1/2 onion, finely chopped
- 4 tbsp. water
- 4 tbsp. chopped walnuts

1. In a large saucepan over medium heat, combine all the ingredients except the walnuts. Bring to a boil and then reduce heat and simmer, uncovered, for 15–20 minutes or until the mixture thickens.
2. Remove from the heat and let cool to room temperature.
3. Cover and refrigerate for up to 2 weeks. Serve at room temperature.

Fig Compote
Makes 1 1/4 cups/250 ml

- 1 (8 oz./225 g) package Calimyrna figs, stemmed and chopped
- 1 3/4 cups/400 ml water
- 3 tbsp. sugar
- 1 tbsp. fresh lemon juice

1. In a small saucepan over medium heat, bring the figs, water, and sugar to a boil. Reduce heat, cover, and simmer for 20–25 minutes or until most of the liquid has been absorbed and the figs are soft.
2. Transfer to a food processor or blender and process until smooth.
3. Transfer to a small bowl and stir in the lemon juice.
4. Cover and refrigerate for up to 2 weeks. Serve at room temperature.

Candied Pecans

- 3 tbsp. Karo (light corn syrup)
- 1 1/2 tbsp. sugar
- 3/4 tsp. salt
- 1/2 tsp. freshly ground black pepper
- 1/8 tsp. cayenne pepper
- 1 1/2 cups/350 g pecan halves

1. Preheat the oven to 325°F. Spray a baking sheet with nonstick cooking spray.
2. In a large bowl, combine all the ingredients. Stir well to coat the nuts and then transfer to the prepared pan.
3. Bake for 5 minutes and then stir with a fork to distribute the coating. Bake for 8–10 minutes more or until pecans are lightly browned and the coating is bubbling.
4. Transfer to another baking sheet and quickly separate the nuts before letting cool completely.
5. Store in an airtight tin for up to 2 weeks.

Celtic Golf & Quinlan Tours

is pleased to announce

FLAVORS OF IRELAND
13-Day Escorted Tour

with

MARGARET M. JOHNSON

Enjoy the best of Irish food and drink; visit cheese makers, salmon smokers, farmers' markets; tour historic and cultural venues; experience a lively weekend in Dublin; stay in five-star and deluxe accommodations; play optional rounds of golf at Doonbeg, Lough Erne, and Old Head of Kinsale.

Overnight stays at Doonbeg Lodge, Co. Clare; Ballynahinch Castle, Recess, Co. Galway; Solis Lough Eske Castle, Co. Donegal; Lough Erne Resort, Enniskillen, Co. Fermanagh; The Merrion Hotel, Dublin; Perryville House, Kinsale, Co. Cork; and Killarney Park Hotel, Killarney, Co. Kerry

Highlights

Visits and Admissions to Cliffs of Moher, Slieve League Cliffs, Kylemore Abbey, Knock Shrine, Rock of Cashel, Belleek Pottery, Triona Design, Blarney Castle Walking Tours of Galway, Dublin, Kinsale Open-Top Bus Tour of Dublin Tour and Tasting at Guinness Storehouse or Jameson Distillery Optional Spa Visits Optional Golf

Tour Includes

Group transfers on arrival and departure
Sightseeing by luxury coach throughout
11 full Irish breakfasts
3 drinks receptions
9 dinners, including 6 table d'hote dinners, Merry Ploughman Pub and Show in Dublin, seafood dinner at Fishy Fishy Café in Kinsale
Signed copy of *Flavors of Ireland* by Margaret M. Johnson

For details, dates, and pricing

www.celticgolf.com or *www.quinlantours.com*

800-535-6148

Go where Ireland *takes you*
Call 800 SHAMROCK or visit discoverireland.com

GLOSSARY

BACON, LOIN OF

Much like smoked pork shoulder in taste, a loin of bacon is a thick slab of pork taken from the belly of a pig. It is the meat used in the traditional Irish dish known as Bacon and Cabbage.

BACON, TRADITIONAL IRISH

Irish bacon is less fatty than American-style bacon and less crispy when cooked. When sliced thin and served as part of an Irish breakfast, the bacon strips are known as *rashers*.

BANGERS

Bangers are sausages made of ground pork and breadcrumbs. They are used in Coddle, a casserole of sausage and potatoes, or served with mashed potatoes. Bangers are an integral part of an Irish breakfast.

BLACK PUDDING

Black pudding is a sausage made of ground pork, spices, oatmeal, and pork blood, which gives it its distinctive color. Black pudding is traditionally served as part of an Irish breakfast.

DIGESTIVE BISCUITS

These semi-sweet crackers are often served with tea; they are also used in crumbs for cheesecake.

FARMHOUSE CHEESE

Surprisingly, cheese was never a mainstay of the Irish diet, even in a country so full of cattle grazing in rich pastures. In the late 1970s, however, the European art of cheese making began to be practiced by a handful of farmers who saw it as a way to use up excess milk. They formed a group known as Cáis (Irish Farmhouse Cheesemakers Association) in 1983 and now boast over 100 members.

GOOD FOOD IRELAND

This organization promotes places to stay, eat, cook, and shop that are committed to the support and use of local Irish and artisan food producers. Founded by Margaret Jeffares in 2006, the group now includes more than 200 members who regularly take part in food showcases, e-marketing and direct marketing campaigns, and other forums that promote Irish food and drink.

IRISH WHISKEY

Irish whiskey undergoes a triple distillation process and a three-year maturation period that distinguishes its flavor from that of Scotch whiskey. Single malts, like Knappogue Castle, are unblended whiskeys produced in a single distillery from malted barley.

MEAD

Once the drink of the ancient Gauls and Anglo-Saxons, who made it from fermented honey and water, today mead is made in Bunratty, Co. Clare, from white wine, honey, and herbs. Known as Bunratty Meade, it is served as a welcoming drink at the famous medieval castle banquets.

Oat cakes

These crisp, savory biscuits are made with oatmeal and water and served with cheese.

Smoked salmon

Irish salmon is salted, dried, and then smoked over an open wood fire or in a kiln either horizontally on trays or suspended over an oak or beech wood fire.

White pudding

A sausage made of ground pork, spices, and oatmeal, it is traditionally served as part of an Irish breakfast.

Food, Drink, and Tourism Websites

Bewley Irish Imports
www.bewleyirishimports.com

Castle Brands
www.castlebrandsinc.com; www.knappoguewhiskey.com

Celtic Golf & Quinlan Tours
www.celticgolf.com, www.quinlantours.com

Cork Butter Museum
www.corkbutter.museum

Ditty's Home Bakery
www.dittysbakery.com

Farmers' Markets in Ireland
www.bordbia.ie

Fermanagh Black Bacon
www.blackbacon.com

Good Food Ireland
www.goodfoodireland.ie

Irish Dairy Board (Kerrygold)
www.kerrygold.com

Irish Farmhouse Cheesemakers Association (Cáis)
www.irishcheese.ie

Irish Food Board
www.bordbia.ie

Lily O'Brien's Chocolate Café
www.lilyscafenyc.com

Lough Erne Resort
www.lougherneresort.com

Magners Irish Cider
www.magners.ie

McCann's Irish Oatmeal
www.mccanns.ie

McGeough Craft Butchers

www.connemarafinefoods.ie

Restaurant Association of Ireland

www.rai.ie

Shannon Heritage

www.shannonheritage.com

Solis Lough Eske Castle Hotel

www.solishotels.com

Taste of Ulster

www.tasteofulster.org

Tommy Moloney's Irish Meats

www.tommymoloneys.com

Tourism in Ireland

www.discoverireland.com

INDEX

C

R

S

Photo courtesy of Lough Erne Resort

FOR MORE INFORMATION ABOUT
Margaret Johnson
&
Flavors of Ireland
please visit:

www.irishcook.com
www.margaretmjohnson.com
Facebook: Margaret Johnson
eirecook@yahoo.com

....

For more information about
AMBASSADOR INTERNATIONAL
please visit:

www.ambassador-international.com
@AmbassadorIntl
www.facebook.com/AmbassadorIntl